Swaying

ESSAYS ON INTERCULTURAL LOVE

Edited by
Jessie Carroll Grearson
and Lauren B. Smith

University of Iowa Press

Iowa City

University of Iowa Press,

Iowa City 52242

Copyright © 1995 by the

University of Iowa Press

Printed in the United States of America

Design by Richard Hendel

Printed on acid-free paper

Library of Congress Cataloging-in-Publication Data

Swaying: essays on intercultural love / edited by Jessie

Carroll Grearson and Lauren B. Smith.

p.   cm.

ISBN 0-87745-526-0,

ISBN 0-87745-527-9 (paper)

1. Intercountry marriage — Case studies.   2. Interethnic

dating — Case studies.   3. Married women — Case

studies.   I. Grearson, Jessie Carroll.   II. Smith, Lauren B.

HQ1032.S93   1995

306.84′5—dc20   95-33941

CIP

01   00   99   98   97   96   95   C   5   4   3   2   1
01   00   99   98   97   P   5   4   3   2

For

our first families,

who taught us

to dream about

a wider world,

and for

our new

international families,

who have

invited us into

their worlds.

CONTENTS

ENDURING

ACKNOWLEDGMENTS

Our first thanks to Mary Swander for being
an excellent mentor. Thank you to Corinne Morrissey,
Marian Staats, and Arlynne Grearson for reading drafts of
the book. We'd also like to express our appreciation to
the contributors for their hard work and belief in the
importance of this project and to Holly Carver for being
a wonderful editor and so darn nice about everything.
Thank you to the John Marshall Law School for help and
support.
Finally, our love and thanks to Hassimi Traore and to
Viren Sapat, who provided endless patience and
technical support.

SWAYING:
AN INTRODUCTION

n American who forms an intercultural relationship must be prepared to be looked at, especially if she is white and her partner is almost seven feet tall and from the dry earth of equatorial Africa. If her husband is East Indian, she must be prepared to be listened to in restaurants where the tables are close together, where people leave deliberate lulls in conversation to hear what each partner orders, especially if one voice is inflected with the lilt of an Indian accent. People in intercultural relationships must be prepared for extra attention, some of it subtle and some of it not so subtle.

Lauren: Hassimi and I get out of the car at a rest stop in Kentucky on our way to the beach in North Carolina, and there is a palpable

change. In the Midwest, people are curious about us, but here people stare, and there is an undercurrent of hostility. I slide my hand into Hassimi's and speak to him in French. Let them get it all at once, the interracial and the international; put everything on the table so they don't stay curious long. North Carolina is better. I still feel people's eyes on us, but things seem safe, even friendly. At the beach, with my mother and some of her friends, we are walking back to the cottage. We have been swimming in the salt water for hours. The dunes are glowing gold behind us and the grass is blown flat by the wind. My mother's friend takes a picture of us. In the picture, we look happy. I am tan and squinting; Hassimi is a shade darker than usual. Behind us in the picture, a woman has stopped in her tracks. She has turned to watch us walk away. Her gaping— it is not hostile—is caught. She gapes at us forever, in a small plastic frame on my bookcase.

Jessie: Viren and I are on Devon Avenue, walking down the street and suddenly it turns from suburban Chicago to Little India. Indians everywhere, especially women, in bright-colored clothes and orange-gold jewelry that I know is real. But what I most feel are the eyes, shining black eyes that look and look at us as we walk. Here there is not the quick, self-conscious glance of Americans, who look at us and look away, smiling off into the distance after our eyes meet. Even if I smile at these Indian women, they look back expressionlessly, continue their inspection. Especially older women whose white hair is streaked the faded pink of henna, and I imagine that they are judging me, and I know that Viren was right to gently detach his brown fingers from my pink ones. We escape into a grocery store, but I still feel like a blanched leaf, drifting along behind him. I keep my voice low as we discuss the things we need, and I watch people watch with interest as we select doodhi and dals and packages marked with names becoming familiar to me.

But *we* look at other couples, too. It is both curiosity, for us, and the desire to connect. We want to know what it means to them, whether or not it is difficult, what they worry about, what they fight about. We want to know whether or not they have children, what those children look like, how they celebrate holidays, what languages they speak. We are like you, we want to say. *When we go to Jewel, our neighborhood grocery store, sometimes Viren leans over the cart and whispers "ICR"—his code word for intercultural relationship. I try to look discreetly at his new find. There is always a surprise. At this grocery store, we often see older couples. I imagine what it must have been like a generation ago. It must have been difficult.* But we cannot breach the barriers that divide strangers in American grocery stores; we cannot march up to them and ask them the questions we want to ask. Instead, we hear a woman speaking French to a man in Nikes and we strain in their direction, move closer to the lettuce, pretend to examine it intently.

Long before we began to collect the essays for this book, we searched for images like these, hungry for stories of other people who had made similar commitments across cultural lines, who had moved, to use Gerald Graff's phrase, "beyond the culture wars." How did other people struggle through the large and small questions that such relationships continually raise? How did they celebrate their choices, their lives together? Over time, we found plenty of anecdotal information; we made friends, connections, heard gossip. We also found a number of sociological texts that gave us technical names for stages and made stark predictions about the dilemmas people in such relationships face.

The discrepancy between the anecdotes and the sociological prose fed a suspicion, soon a growing conviction, that the subject of intercultural relationships had not been sufficiently explored. There were two voices telling us very different things. The scientific "we" of the sociologists had a distanced, objectifying tone, made the couples seem faraway, "problematic." The "we" of the couples themselves was more complicated and more poignant. While sociologists asked, "How do intercultural couples deal with cultural and religious conflicts?" people in these relationships asked, "Who will make me chapatis by hand?"

and "Who will teach my children the songs of Ramadan?" While the sociologists asked, "How will couples cope with parental disapproval?" people in relationships asked, "Who will take care of my mother?" The sociologists see these relationships as an interesting subject to be studied; the couples see them as ongoing attempts to be happy.

We wanted to collect essays that filled the gap between anecdotes that came to us in fragments and sociological studies that pinned down, labeled, and categorized intercultural relationships. We wanted to find beautiful, complicated prose that reflected the creative potential of choosing diversity, that explored in many voices the social, cultural, and spiritual consequences of this choice. Especially, we wanted prose that could do two things at once: acknowledge the sometimes anguishingly difficult, sometimes unsolvable, dilemmas of intercultural couples *and* celebrate the creative solutions that many couples find.

What we have suspected from the start, and what is echoed in the essays in this anthology, is that people survive and thrive through complicated movements between spaces, places, and beliefs. Intercultural relationships live in the world of what we have come to call the "radical *and*"—a place where multiple cultures find expression. That is, intercultural couples find themselves choosing not to choose between their own cultures of origin; instead, they move among cultures, between struggles and harmony, accepting what they can and negotiating what they cannot, articulating what they can and trusting the inarticulable to somehow make itself known.

We turned to the literary essay as a vehicle for the "radical *and*," a way of replacing the "this *or* that" with the "this *and* that" of intercultural relationships, a way of having multiple worlds instead of having to choose among them. We chose the literary essay because such essays have at their center a paradox, some tension, some or several questions tugging back and forth at the attention of the writer. Each involves both paradox and conviction, both conflict and uneasy, provisional resolution. Each somehow captures a hint that the human condition is itself somehow paradoxical, that it never will rest easily or triumph with a particular right answer.

"Essay" literally means an attempt, a try. Part of the essay, the impulse to try, is to keep trying. It's built into the verb. To try implies an ongoing attempt, that the essayist writes right off the page, walks away still talking to herself or to us, still questioning. Not fictional, but not a simple personal account, the essay moves back and forth from sight into blindness, from the certain to the uncertain, in an attempt to grapple with what always lies outside of familiar experience. The essay does what intercultural couples must do; it lives the questions, forges a crooked path between known and unknown territories.

Our title, *Swaying*, suggests both the problem, the instability of these intercultural relationships, and its provisional solution, flexibility. It suggests a bending between different realities, different worlds, a movement that is graceful but suggests uncertainty, insecurity, even trouble. A tree sways in a storm. We sway with the music. We allow ourselves to be swayed. Our title suggests the kind of multiple movement that the renegotiation of boundaries requires — both swaying and being swayed, the ability to be flexible while remaining rooted in our own cultural identities.

We made several decisions in planning this book, and one of them was the decision to define "intercultural" provisionally, as involving two people from different countries and cultures who may also, though not always, differ in religion or race. This choice was largely an arbitrary one, reflecting our need to draw some boundaries around our project. The term intercultural is often used ambiguously. It can mean — interchangeably — interracial, interreligious, or interethnic. While we recognize the importance of all these versions of "intercultural," we thought it was important to provide a collection of writings that specifically addressed the problems of couples who choose each other across national boundaries.

International couples have to deal with historical and cultural differences that, if they are not different in kind, may at least differ in degree from those faced by interracial and interreligious couples who share a national identity. American couples of any race or religion share at least some cultural knowledge. We, however, cannot assume much of anything but the goodwill of our partners, who may not know what we're talking about when we talk about MASH, Dr. Seuss, or the Wizard of Oz. They might not understand our feelings about the necessity of toasters, the desirability of front porches or backyards. We, on the other hand, might not know the unspeakable rudeness of sending our skivvies out with the rest of the laundry or kissing in public. We may misinterpret the meaning of closed and open doors — or silence. By isolating the international facet of "intercultural," we hope to shed light on the more inclusive uses of the term, while focusing on an aspect of "intercultural" that is particularly neglected.

This project also shares common ground with multicultural writing and with travel writing, but again there are some important differences. Travel writers typically narrate their developing sense of self in the context of a culture that they perceive as foreign, while multicultural writers generally articulate their allegiance to a single ethnic or international identity in the context of a mainstream culture that perceives them as foreign. In either case, the writers are concerned with setting up boundaries between the self and the other. In contrast, the essays in *Swaying* attempt to renegotiate boundaries, to imagine a life that can contain two or more cultures without erasing any.

Our provisional attempts to define "intercultural" are lodged in even more complicated, and sometimes painful, questions that are an important part of this book. When we discussed this project with colleagues and friends, nearly everyone wanted to explain how their relationship could be included as "intercultural." For example, one of our colleagues offered to write an essay on his intercultural relationship with his cat. This is by far the most original proposal we received, but in spirit was very similar to many other responses. People, if not necessarily resistant to our definition, pushed us to expand it. *My relationship is*

intercultural because we grew up in different eras. I am rural and
my husband is urban; I am from the North and my wife is from
the South; I am a doctor and my husband is a lawyer. Nearly
everyone insisted that his or her relationship was in some way
intercultural.

Of course, to some degree, they are right. Even people from
different professions develop different vocabularies and different
assumptions about the world, and families develop their own
microculture, their own traditions and vocabularies, their own
expectations and inside jokes. In this sense, all relationships are
intercultural because each couple must form its own unique culture out of two.

We discovered, however, that to ignore the definition of intercultural relationships that we explore in *Swaying* is to overlook
the particular complexities intercultural couples confront, is to
leave unacknowledged the losses people in intercultural relationships suffer, the sweeping historical differences that reach into
the hearts of people who come from different parts of the earth,
who speak different languages. It is a failure to recognize what
is not completely comparable to American-American partner-
ships, what is at least partially outside of other people's ken.

We understand now what other writers mean when they say
that a project "took on a life of its own." As it developed, *Sway-*
ing seemed to dictate some of the choices we made. Initially, for
example, we'd planned to include men's essays, as well as contributions from gay and lesbian writers. The overwhelming major-
ity of proposals we received, however, were from women; and
essays dealing with love for another woman simply did not materialize. In any case, in the body of essays and proposals we
did receive, a surprising coherence of theme and tone emerged.
These are primarily essays about women and men — specifically,
about women struggling to love, understand, or sometimes free
themselves from men whose cultural backgrounds are very different from their own. Many of them, furthermore, are also
about women coping with a sexism difficult to name because
it is refracted through two or more cultural prisms — about

women struggling with culturally prescribed ideas of romance and marriage.

Also, many decisions we made were influenced by our personal odyssey. The project developed out of our readings, curiosity, needs as women involved with men from other parts of the world. A number of the essays included here were contributed by an international network of people who know us, who know friends of ours, who know other contributors. This makes for a perspective loosely circumscribed by our knowledge, experiences, connections. Many contributors, for example, are American women, like us, commenting on their relationships with men from other countries. Obviously, we cannot claim to have provided a range of voices in any way representative of the international community we hope this book speaks to. However, we do feel that the essays in this book comment on each other in enlightening ways.

This book is meant to initiate a conversation that needs to be elaborated on. We hope that these essays work together to recomplicate issues that tend to get flattened — especially by Americans who often think of themselves as open-minded and as part of a relatively successful multicultural society. These essays remind us again and again of how complex things continue to be: gender issues are entangled with cultural issues, cultural issues are entangled with issues of personal history, personal history is always both cultural and gendered. In the end, perhaps the refusal of simple answers is the most characteristic gesture of the essays included here.

Lauren: I tell my cousin, who is American, that my African partner is always working in the lab, that he doesn't find very much time for fun. I tell her I feel frustrated and confused. "Oh," she says, "he is a 'workaholic,'" a very American expression. "Well," I say, but I am caught. Should I explain to her the years of struggle in an overburdened African school and then again in an American higher education system not very friendly to "foreigners"? His single-

mindedness cannot be understood as an addiction; it is a necessity. "No," I finally say, "it is not that simple."

Jessie: I tell my American friend that I agreed to pose for a picture to be sent back to India. In the picture I stand, enfolded in a silk sari, pretending to spoon food out of an empty bowl onto my relatives' plates as they smile up at me, the good maniben, housewife. "You," she said, "have given in to your husband's sexist culture." "Yes," I think, "this is true"—and then, remembering how everyone sprang up after the photograph to help prepare the actual food, do the actual dishes, "no, it is more complicated than that."

These are the kinds of complications *Swaying* explores. Clearly, these are not just stories about food or clothing or funny mistakes. But sometimes they *are* stories about food and clothing and funny mistakes. We've come to understand that none of these issues is small, that questions about food, colors, clothing, housework, holidays are almost always connected to larger ones. *What will we eat for dinner?* becomes *Who will make me sima and milk when I am sick? Where shall we live?* becomes *Who will spend time with my parents when they are old? What should I wear?* becomes *Will his family accept me as one of their own?*

We organized this book as a multivoiced narrative with three sections reflecting the development of intercultural relationships from a preoccupation with "small" issues to a deeper understanding of the large issues always embedded in the small. The first section explores the early phases of commitment, of connecting with another. Attention in these essays is generally fixed on the lover himself, a fascination with the ways he embodies the culture he comes from and a negotiation of the differences that arise in the course of everyday life.

The essays in the second section are more panoramic in their scope: their focus widens to include children and grandparents, multiple landscapes and family histories. For example, Le Ly Hayslip's breathless description of her first encounter with her

American in-laws juxtaposes starkly different Vietnamese and American attitudes toward kinship. Hayslip, missing her own mother, wonders why her mother-in-law didn't "move in with her daughter, who had more than enough room. . . . I guessed that Americans loved their possessions so much that even a lonely old woman valued her own TV set, kitchen, bathroom, spare bedrooms, and garage for a car she couldn't drive more than living with a daughter in her sunset years." Fern Kupfer, in contrast, lays her husband's Lebanese family traditions alongside her own Jewish-American ones, insisting upon the similarities arising from their long-entangled histories: "My husband and I both come from a place where parents are in the habit of intensely observing their children, where it is not possible to come into a room without having one's appearance commented upon. A belt improperly looped. A stooped shoulder. A pimple on the forehead. All were fodder for interpretation and advice. . . . A kind of well-meaning busybodiness that characterized both our homes and separated us from the more emotionally remote families — the ones my family called 'goyisha,' what Joe's referred to as 'Amerkani.' "

The third section, "Enduring," we find to be at once the most somber *and* the most hopeful. These essays explore both meanings of the word "endure." They are about what it means to bear burdens, to cope with difficulties, but they are also about what lasts. These essays grapple with highly dramatic subjects: death, divorce, alienation from one's original homeland, as well as the creation of viable, even successful hybrid cultures. Interestingly, the writers included in the third section turn back to an examination of the self, find a deeply personal way to deal with seemingly unreconcilable realities: for Catherine Casale and Susan Tiberghien, this is a more or less graceful fitting together of mosaic pieces from multiple cultures; for Nora Egan and Lita Page, it is a wrenching decision to return, though not unmarked, to their original cultures; for Ruth Prawer-Jhabvala, it is a more resigned straddling of two worlds she does not hope to bring together.

She writes, "And here, it seems to me, I come to the heart of my problem. To live in India and be at peace, one must to a very considerable extent become Indian and adopt Indian attitudes, habits, beliefs, assume if possible an Indian personality. But how is this possible? And even if it were possible — without cheating oneself — would it be desirable? Should one want to become other than what one is? I don't always say no to this question. Sometimes it seems to me how pleasant it would be to say yes and give in and wear a sari and be meek and accepting and see God in a cow. Other times it seems worthwhile to be defiant and European and — all right, be crushed by one's environment, but all the same to have made some attempt to remain standing. Of course, this can't go on indefinitely, and in the end I'm bound to lose — if only at the point where my ashes are immersed in the Ganges to the accompaniment of Vedic hymns, and then who will say that I have not truly merged with India?"

Reading these essays and writing our own has helped us begin to sort out the nature of our own intercultural relationships — helped us better understand Indian, African, and American cultures as well as our own unique interpretations of those cultures. Trying to pinpoint and write about such distinctions — the unique and personal in dialogue with the common and cultural — seems to us at the heart of true intercultural understanding, an understanding that seeks to appreciate differences without stereotyping. Finding this balance continues to be one of America's most pressing projects and deepest needs.

onnecting

DISHES
ON THE
DRAINBOARD

Christi Merrill

 have three hours to finish my article before the Federal Express office closes and it's dinnertime. Kishan is downstairs waiting for me to make something to eat. We can't eat until I make dinner and I can't make dinner until the counters are clear and the counters won't be clear until the dishes in the sink are clean and I am too frantic to take the time to throw the fit to make him feel guilty enough to do the dishes so we can sit down and eat.

Kishan categorically refuses to do dishes. Something about his masculinity and I-am-an-Indian-man-after-all. I could tell him I am an American woman after all and I have a deadline to meet besides, but he is as suspicious of being forced to play the part of American husband as I am of playing Indian wife. At this point I don't trust many aspects of his culture, and he doesn't trust many in mine. And yet here we are in this relationship, still, drawn to each other somehow.

He's downstairs watching the MacNeil/Lehrer NewsHour now, with the volume turned low. He made a snack for himself an hour ago so he could wait patiently, without disturbing me. I heard him open the pantry door, heard him rinsing off something at the sink, heard silverware clattering. Sweet, buttery smells came from the kitchen. His quiet way of waiting is meant to prove that he encourages my writing. That he respects my American side. He tiptoes around the house and irons his shirts himself before he goes off in the morning. "Don't get up, I'll make my own tea," he said today when he got home from work. He looked at my back bent over the keyboard and waited for me to say, "Thank you."

These are the ways we disappoint each other. These are the ways we become failures in each other's eyes. He smiles and nods over my shoulder as he reads the last paragraph I've written, and then looks pointedly at the laundry basket in the corner, overflowing with smelly clothes. His thick, dark eyebrows rise on his forehead. He thinks to himself that the balance I hope for myself is impossible, that I will never be a success as a writer and still be able to maintain a sane, happy home. "I could if my husband did his fair share," I retort, silently, arching my own eyebrows. I turn toward the overflowing laundry basket, too, and pick out *his* pair of pants, *his* dirty socks, with my eyes. "Yours, yours, yours," I want my look to say.

We each try to pretend we don't hear these unarticulated accusations. His silent reprobations have become a voice in my head, telling me that I shouldn't be reading this book when the bed still hasn't been made, that I shouldn't continue to work at my computer when guests may drop by, or when dinner needs to be made, or when the floors need to be swept, or when any little thing in the house is dirty or out of place.

In a house, I know, there is always something dirty or out of place.

I try hanging curtains in front of messes, throwing blankets over piles. I try closing doors. But my outrage with the clutter grows to distracting proportions even when I am diligently ignoring it. Outrage not just with the clutter but with the thought that half of the housework generated between two people cannot be divided equally in a simple mathematical equation. A day multiplied by the two of us makes forty-eight hours, but the time I get for writing seems like such a small amount in comparison.

Kishan says he doesn't believe that our life together should be reduced to such simple equations. Numbers are too stark, counting too petty. He recounts scenes from his childhood home in the dreamy, lyrical way he has with words that first made me fall in love with him: of his brothers and sisters waking before sunrise and bathing in cold water out of a bucket, his mother sweeping out the courtyard with a whiskbroom, her voice straining as she sang twilight devotional hymns to the goddess. You could be happy, too, he says, if you would stop calculating everything in life in these puny numbers. He is using his jokey voice, and I am touched to have his full attention turned on me. "You're a writer, not a vegetable seller!" he adds, and I can't stop laughing.

I met Kishan in his village when I had gone there to interview his uncle for a magazine article on the relationship of folk traditions to his short stories. As a fellow writer, I was immediately brought into the men's world. Every morning I walked to the office with the men and sat all day at a large wooden desk while we worked. I walked back home with the men at noon after one of the children had come dashing up the hill to announce shyly and proudly that dinner was ready. A thrill shuddered through the house as our contingent announced its arrival with an insistent thud on the heavy, brass-worked wooden door.

We sat ourselves down on cushiony aqua-tinted vinyl armchairs in a sunny parlor and enjoyed the spring desert breeze as the children began to run in plates full of food the women had spent the morning preparing. Sweetish, sourish mustard greens cooked over a cow-dung flame; creamy lentils hot with local red peppers; smooth, fatty yoghurt made from buffalo milk; and thick millet chapatis baked over twigs scavenged from the sparse countryside. As the guest, I was served first, along with the patriarch of the household. Children sprinted from the kitchen to the parlor to offer us hot chapatis the moment our supply threatened exhaustion, to spoon seconds of lentils, mustard greens, yoghurt, into our half-empty steel bowls. It wasn't bad to be a man in India, after all.

Was I to believe their assurances that the women were happy to go to such trouble for us? "This is the life they've chosen for themselves," I was told, as if pulling a veil down in front of one's face and spending eight hours a day grinding flour and scouring spice grease off dishes inside a dimly lit, smoky kitchen were the natural result of marital union. These women chose not to defy their parents and so were married. These women have chosen to obey their in-laws, every day for the rest of their lives — don't sit on the front porch where the neighbors might see your face, it will bring shame upon our family; last night your ankles were showing as you slept, have you no dignity; why are you in here reading a magazine, haven't you seen the courtyard, it's absolute confusion; bow to this uncle, bow to that aunt, have sons sons sons, daughters only suck money.

I imagine myself waking in this same house day after day — to light the hearth fire and sweep out the rooms — and I am filled with a hollow despair as I think ahead to the end of each day, when I have to give some sort of account to myself. Is it because I have been taught only to value what has traditionally been considered men's work that a day spent cooking and cleaning feels like a waste? Why do I assume that the long hours I put into researching a magazine article are preferable to the long hours the women of the house put into preparing our food? Would they even want to live my life if given the choice? Would I really be so unhappy with theirs?

I ask myself these questions because I know, at heart, that the regular rhythm of Indian life seduces me. Wake at dawn with the sun a red sliver on the scrubby, sandy horizon. Cook vegetables fresh from the garden, wholesome pulses and grains, deep-colored spices, turmeric yellow, chili-pepper red, cumin brown. The splash of cool water on warm concrete as you wash the dirty clothes. The shallow, moist breathing sounds of a child you have just put down to sleep. In India it is considered a sign of status if you can afford to let your women remain at home all day without having to step outside to work. A sign of status for whom? I ignore the larger questions and indulge my fantasies of a life without Federal Express deadlines, without rent to pay or subways to catch. No deadlines, no rent to pay, no trains to catch, would I ever get any writing done?

I'm getting hungry now and begin to think in extremes. I want to steal into the kitchen and grab a handful of raw oats and raisins. Frozen peas. Anything I can eat quick and easy, without turning on the oven or washing plates. Uncooked egg noodles. Chocolate chips. Peanut butter. I don't want Kishan to hear me. He sneers whenever he sees me reduced to this: out of control, disheveled.

We should have gone grocery shopping days ago, but I was already in a panic about the article when we ran out of bread and milk. The last time I had a deadline frenzy I saw it coming and made a pot of refried beans to last the week. We would stand at the counter whenever I took breaks, dipping tortilla chips into the beans, crunching wildly, and trading stories of what happened to us that day. We kept smiling at each other, fresh coriander and garlic on our tongues, relieved that the tension hadn't built up, that our life was still going on.

The night I sent off that article, Kishan and I lay side by side in the darkness talking of life here, remembering life there. The more time we spend in India, he assures me, the happier I will be. The best thing for a writer, he tells me, is a regular routine. "Isn't it, my little vegetable seller," he teases. He is teasing me, but by the tone of his voice I know this deadline has upset his equilibrium, refried beans or no. "You could be happy, too," he reassures me, "if you would slow down and enjoy." He begins talking about his mother in the misty way he has when he's feeling most uncertain, of her laying her hand on his forehead whenever he was sick, of her sending him special sesame-seed sweets she had prepared when he was away at school. Her twilight prayers to the goddess, her milking the cows, baking the bread, morning, evening, morning, evening, as regular as the rise and set of the sun.

It's the sudden distance between us, the sudden silence in the house, that bothers him most. The women he grew up with are as steady as heartbeats, filling buckets with fresh water when the spigots turn on, shaking out the sheets, sweeping the floors, washing the clothes. I am amazed that his mother can sustain the momentum of an entire family, day after day, without feeling depressed or resentful. A vital organ keeping all the life forces of their household coursing along track — she is the heart of their home. I say simply that she gives much to those around her and am about to add —

But Kishan finishes my sentence for me. "Doing all this makes her very happy," he says, with so much bitterness I cannot tell him that I had meant to say that, too. He doesn't believe I understood this. Doesn't believe that part of me wants this kind of life, also. He describes to me how content his mother is, suddenly propping himself up on his elbow so that he can look directly into my eyes and read my reactions by distant streetlight. He tells me how the satisfaction of being interdependent with others outweighs any other satisfaction; we are not scavenging jackals to live alone and die alone, we are human beings.

He does not understand that I also want to be interdependent, but I want to find a new way to balance the workload. I try to explain this to him in Hindi and realize I do not even know the word for "equal." When I buy vegetables in the bazaars, I calculate sums on a more tangible level — this many classes per week per semester gives me so many months longer to stay. Are my American dollars really "equal" to the number of rupees that are a meal's worth of okra? Are my English lessons "equal" to the dinners the mothers of these children prepare for me? At times I undersell myself and at others balk at the thought of paying a rickshaw-pedaller or a sweeper so little.

Equal is a word I do not know in Hindi because it represents a level of abstraction that must be translated into practical terms to have any bearing on the life I live. Equal is a balance I have to negotiate every single day, with every person I come into contact with, in a give-and-take, tug-of-war bargaining ritual. I play this tug of war with Kishan, as well, with Kishan most particularly, and have realized that the goal of this game should not be to upset your opponent, but to be sure that he can keep his balance as surely as you can keep yours. To do well in this game you must respond to every subtle shift the other person makes, anticipate your own alterations of position so as not to catch the other unaware, and find a rhythm between the two of you that allows you to settle back into your weight in a counterbalance that is intuitive, spontaneous, comfortable, even. We've been leaning back, trusting the weight of the other to keep our balance. Holding our hands tight. Then I let go suddenly. Of course he's scared of falling.

Kishan may argue with me, he may fight with me, but whenever I reach out he is still there. I've never been afraid of falling. But the more Kishan talks, the less I trust him to allow me to find a position I find most natural. The more he talks, the more I see what he waits for as he waits. I am beginning to worry that Kishan seeks stability based on a formula he will never want to exchange.

With Kishan I talk as if there were neat, clean lines separating his attitude from mine: American versus Indian, North versus South. Our rhetoric has become polarized. But Kishan's voice that says housework is the woman's responsibility echoes the voices I heard growing up, in my father's romantic accounts of threshing and hunting and midday dinners at the farm, in my grandmother's nostalgia for the rhythm of her mother's warm, sweet-smelling kitchen. I struggle to discount these voices, and yet I continue to judge myself by them. If I don't play by their rules, that simple, beautiful way of life will be lost to me completely.

I long for a past that I began to dream of listening to the stories of my grandmother, my father, my great-uncle: waking up in a house you've built yourself on land full of tenacious wildflowers and century-old shade trees, picking fresh tomatoes and string beans from your kitchen garden out back, the entire family gathering in the kitchen three times a day for meals, playing card games at night by lamplight in warm circles of familiarity and laughter, slipping into deep, satisfied sleep each night. My great-grandmother I only knew as a bespectacled, purple-lidded woman who baked buttermilk biscuits and roast chicken for us on holidays. After dinner she would ease her slight, brittle frame into a worn corduroy Lazy-boy rocker near the Ben Franklin stove and smile as she watched us charging past in enthusiastic packs. My grandmother told me her mother knew all the names and birthdates of the grandchildren and great-grand-children, whose pictures she tucked into ingenious nooks in her china cabinet.

Grandma often said she wanted to die just like her mother did, in her sleep, peacefully. The way my grandmother talked, it seemed she thought her mother died contented and peaceful because she lived that way, too. But I would like to go back and ask her now whether she ever had doubts about the life she had chosen for herself, or felt that her expectations for herself were in conflict with the expectations others had of her. Did she resent the amount of work she had to do each day to keep the family running? Did she ever wish she had time to do something else, something creative, something perhaps utterly indulgent?

I sit at the computer feeling ashamed that I am not at the sink. I am determined to ignore the dishes sitting on the drainboard waiting for me, because it is simply not fair and, once I start pandering to these expectations, I will never get any writing done. I get little writing done anyway, since I am too busy arguing in my head. Every sentence I write has to make its way through the stacks of milk-sticky bowls, past cutting boards full of toast crumbs and cheese crusts and the week-old omelette scum left on the skillet, past the drinking glasses mildewing in cold, garlicky dishwater, before it finally burbles up into my head, then down my arms through my fingers to be typed onto the computer screen. It's a long journey my poor sentence has to make. How can Kishan possibly be taken in by this ruse of mine — that I'm ignoring it all, that I have my mind's door shut so I can concentrate on matters more important than dishes?

I hope Kishan is sitting downstairs this moment trying to ignore my voice inside his head. I hope he feels restless and terribly, terribly guilty. He won't, though, I know. He has very clear ideas about how the work between us is divided.

He tells me stories about the Indian men he knows who do dishes, and his voice drops an octave. He uses guttural words from his native Rajasthani to explain how very odd, how very *feminine* these husbands are who squat at the courtyard spigot working layers of oil and spices off plates and pots with mud. A man's work, of course, is outside the home. He digs irrigation ditches and chops firewood. Men who let their wives bully them into doing dishes are men who let themselves be cuckolded. "Doing too many dishes can make a man's dick fall off," I tease. He laughs, too, and looks down at his pants to check.

Kishan doesn't understand where I have seized upon the conviction that housework should be shared evenly between men and women. He never saw my father even clear his plate when we visited there. And after a two-month stay at my aunt and uncle's house he came to the conclusion that a man may contribute to the housekeeping by paying an unassuming woman to clean toilets and vacuum every other week. Where did I get these ideas indeed? Kishan conjectures. Maybe I just don't care enough to take time out for cleaning? Maybe all my talk of equality is just an excuse for a very basic and childish reaction to having to do physical labor: that I simply hate housework. Or that I don't notice.

It's true that I am repulsed by washing dishes and resent having to wash huge mounds of stinky clothing by hand. But I like nothing better than to wake up in a bedroom where all the clothes are neatly folded and the books tucked tidily in place. To me, clean cotton sheets are one of the world's great pleasures. I love to go padding around on recently swept and mopped floors with the sunlight brightening the polish of the stone tile. No matter how many sleazy men have called me darling and tried to touch my bottom out on the Indian streets, if I come home to a kitchen where the erratic daily supply of "fresh" water from the spigot has been collected in a clean bucket ready for cooking, and there are plenty of lentils, rice, and wheat flour on hand, a stash of onions, ginger, garlic, and a spice container full of turmeric, cumin, coriander, red pepper, salt, and perhaps some cloves and bay leaves, and if, of course, the dishes from the previous meal have been cleaned and wait neatly stacked in a corner by the tap, and the counters and floor have been wiped, then I find nothing more relaxing than to spend a few hours cooking up rice and dal, frying up some spicy okra, rolling out chapati after chapati and baking them over the fire on the iron tawa. But who has time to orchestrate such elaborate performances?

Kishan says what I really need is an Indian wife. He says this because he is afraid I am trying to make him into one. "It's wonderful living next door to a feminist," he tells me, talking as if there are twenty strangers listening to our conversation, even though we are alone. "When you live next door to a feminist, you can brag to your friends — look how smart she is! Look how brave she is! How advanced! I would much rather live next door to one than with one. Living with a feminist is too, too much work!" I try to laugh along with him and the invisible twenty men he imagines would find this kind of joke funny, but instead of bringing us closer together, his way of joking only makes me worry that the ideals I thought we once shared were nothing to him but a passing whim. That he doesn't have the commitment necessary to translate these dreams of simplicity, equality, and beauty into day-to-day life. That when it comes to living his life rather than just talking about it, he has other priorities.

Kishan tries to convince me that we should settle in India because that is the place where we will have more time for our writing and filmmaking. "But if I live as your wife, when will I have time for my writing?" I ask him. "Afternoons," he tells me, "that's when the women usually take naps and rest. You can write then." My temper flares. "We can hire a woman to clean our home," he relents. Dishes are not important enough to argue about. We are artists. We should live in a place, he says, where life is calm and beautiful. "Life in an Indian village is calm and beautiful," I say, "precisely because the women work so hard." He thinks once we are back in India I will adjust, will compromise, will step into the rhythm there.

If I were the husband and had an Indian wife, I could enjoy the calmness and beauty of the life without this contradiction. I recognize the daily pleasures and rhythms he describes so lovingly as the India I was captivated by my first few years there as a student, before I ever met Kishan. The fresh, hot milk I drank every night before falling asleep tasted creamy and animalish, like the milk I used to drink at my great-grandfather's farm. The fine layers of soot that collected along the walls where the women cooked smelled like my great-grandmother's kitchen, a smell enhanced by the metallic yellow stain on the glasses left from the minerals in the well water. The women's hands, gentle and competent as they rolled out dough and bent kindling in half, reminded me of my grandmother's, sprinkling chopped walnuts onto Christmas cookies, pressing a cold cloth onto my feverish forehead.

Kishan persists. He tells me stories of the happy women he remembers from his childhood who sang as they scrubbed floors, who spent hours together every afternoon stitching clothes, chaffing wheat, gossiping, laughing. I smile, in frustration, and wish I could be satisfied with such a life. That I wouldn't always be wanting, lacking, something else, something more. Something I'm not sure I will ever have.

"I want a wife, not a house slave," he told his mother once, somewhat indelicately, when she was pressing him with threats and tears to agree to an arranged marriage with a village girl of his caste. Is this what he thinks of when he says I need an Indian wife? I think of my friends, many of whom are, indeed, Indian wives. My friend the journalist who collaborates with her photographer husband on magazine articles. My friend the teacher who started an alternative primary school with her husband, also a teacher. Poets, clothing designers, social activists, professors, I can think of many Indian wives who haven't succumbed to the extreme expectations that would turn them into house slaves. I couldn't make someone a house slave any more than become one myself.

In his village I cringed every time his sisters-in-law insisted on laying out my bedding for me at night or offered to make me tea. Each morning when I walked up the hill away from the house, I stumbled and tripped over stones in the road, worried that I walked with the same self-important, oblivious swagger I saw in the men. Of course, the eyes that saw this swagger were ones I imagined looking out from the house. I was being split into two.

I began to miss the tangible satisfaction of chopping vegetables. Miss knowing where the antiseptic was to treat a child's cut, miss polishing the copper-bottomed pots when I got stuck writing. I was not accustomed to walking so far from the room where I cooked to the room where I wrote. I started to make my own rules that wobbled between the gender lines.

I still went to the office everyday but started sitting with the women in the kitchen when I went home for meals, and rinsing off my own plates when I was finished. A small gesture, really, but the men in his family never sat in the kitchen. It caused great bewilderment at the beginning. The first time I came into the kitchen, their mother-in-law pushed me back out and, when I insisted, ordered Savitri to fetch me a burlap sack to sit on, and eyed me strangely through her thick, black-rimmed glasses that magnified the protruding ovalness of her eyeballs. I plunked down on the floor a few feet from the hearth, with the children on either side of me slurping at the warm milk, while the men sat on their aqua-tinted armchairs, waiting for their food to be brought in and served. I could sense alarm behind the women's polite demonstrations, but they let me sit there just the same, and after a few days it began to feel routine almost. I felt relieved to be in the company of women again, not to be constantly re-minded that I was from the opposite side of the gender line.

But as far as the women of the family were concerned, I moved in the men's world and played by men's rules. They lumbered about in the traditional skirts and blouses, whose great lengths of floral printed polyester forced a slow gracefulness of movement that soothed me to watch, but that I could never tolerate for myself. They tucked and retucked the ends of their veils into their waists as they talked, and pulled the sheer meters of pastel-colored cotton low past their chins whenever they heard footsteps. Whereas I sat modern and nimble in my hand-printed cotton salwar-kurta, loose pants and tunic outfits they said made me look like a television starlet from Delhi. I would never move with the same overlapping rhythms and responsibilities that they shared, nor would I understand the names of festival foods or villages or relatives that made up most of their talk. The women treated me with friendly wariness and curiosity.

They would engage me in bright, fast-paced conversation as they rolled out chapatis, warmed butter, filled water jugs. Often Savitri would double over in laughter at my ridiculously mundane questions about cow-dung fuel and brassieres. Mangala would wait and ask me in her quiet, patient way about life in America, questions I always found unanswerable however much they prodded. Why doesn't your father give you money to come here and study? Whom do you have to take care of with the money you earn? Doesn't he worry about your being so far from home, alone? And then suddenly the bond we had built would be broken, the mutual suspicions and envies revealed. You are

very lucky to travel around the world, Mangala would sigh bit-
terly. You have so much free time for reading and writing. Only
moments before, I had been marveling at the fluidity of her
movements as she poured milk into her son's tumbler, skimmed
off the fat, and rinsed out the empty pot. Only moments before,
I had wanted to be at the heart of a home, to do as she did without conflict.

If I did what *you* do, Mangala once told me, my parents
would never have been able to marry me off.

No, this is the life they've chosen for themselves, the men in
his village reassured me, but later that night, my first in their village, when I remained in the bright parlor after dinner to read,
the young daughters-in-law from the house sent the children to
scout the room for men, and, once they were assured that I was
alone, rushed in, giggling and frenzied with excitement, to ask
me about my country and my life there. I hadn't set foot on
American soil for two years and hardly felt as though I were established there, but in answering their questions — Do I live
with my mother and father? Am I married? When will I? How
far did I get with my education? Do I plan to continue working
as a writer? — I realized that even after three years in India, my
expectations for myself were very American. They told me that
they hadn't been outside the house for weeks, that they hadn't
met anyone from outside the village for months. They seemed
reluctant and even a bit bored answering questions about their
children, their in-laws, the day-to-day details of life in a joint
family in a village. The beauty in life that they longed for seemed
elsewhere, they seemed to say. Their eyes widened in a soulfully
hungry way as I described my favorite museums, described
walks in clean parks, sitting in coffee shops with friends dis-
cussing novels we had read. My descriptions were lively and involved, inspired as I was by the village life they were so tired of.

I began asking them about their schooling, their career aspi-
rations, the homes where they grew up, and was surprised to
find Savitri talking of her job as a Sanskrit teacher that she had

to give up to get married. Suddenly, her eyes were sparkling. My father ordered me to get married, she confided to me, but I am thinking of leaving this village and going back there to work. I asked her if her parents would support her in this decision, but she shook her head, sadly, no.

The next time I went back to the village, she was mysteriously gone, and Mangala looked lonelier and more overburdened than ever. When I asked after her, her husband explained snidely that she couldn't live in a village without her cooler and fridge. I asked after Savitri's career ambitions, her literary inspirations, while he answered in generalizations about modern girls not appreciating the calm and beauty of the village. Mangala just shrugged her shoulders and said, if she were as educated as Savitri, she, too, would go back to her parents' home to work.

But it wasn't long before Savitri's parents insisted she go back to her husband. At least, that was the explanation offered to me. In the year since her return I noticed she had grown even skinnier and more pinched, despite her pregnancy. It was painful to watch her pound the water-heavy, sudsy laundry against the stone slab. When I tried to ask how she felt to be back, she shrugged her shoulders, but I saw in her face that she was becoming bitter and resigned like Mangala. She said she missed wearing salwar-kurtas and jeans sometimes, and riding around on scooters.

Kishan tells me that if we marry and move to his village, I will have to wear a skirt and veil just like Savitri and Mangala. I think to myself, "never." He tells me it would be comfortable, that I will begin to feel embarrassed wearing my salwar-kurtas once I have adapted to life in the village, but I can't imagine adapting that much, crossing the line that far. I keep hoping that we will move beyond these extremes. I want to find a place of mutual respect and understanding that is organic and spontaneous and grows out of our own needs. I am not an Indian wife. Why should I have to live according to formulas I don't believe even Indian women should have to abide?

I get up and creep into the kitchen without turning the lights on. Kishan has done the dishes, quietly, and left them dripping and clean stacked upside-down on the counters. He set some ginger halwa he made out on a plate, hoping I would take a break soon, so I could eat it hot, not wanting to disturb me while I worked.

ADVANCED BIOLOGY

Judith Ortiz Cofer

s I lay out my clothes for the trip to Miami to do a reading from my recently published novel, then on to Puerto Rico to see my mother, I take a close look at my travel wardrobe — the tailored skirts in basic colors easily coordinate with my silk blouses. I have to smile to myself, remembering what my mother had said about my conservative outfits when I visited her the last time — that I looked like the Jehovah's Witnesses who went from door to door in her pueblo trying to sell tickets to heaven to the die-hard Catholics. I would scare people she said. They would bolt their doors if they saw me approaching with my briefcase. As for her, she dresses in tropical colors — a red skirt and parakeet-yellow blouse look good on her tan skin, and she still has a good

enough figure that she can wear a tight black cocktail dress to go dancing at her favorite club, El Palacio, on Saturday nights. And, she emphasizes, still make it to the 10 o'clock mass on Sunday. Catholics can have fun and still be saved, she has often pointed out to me, but only if you pay your respects to God and all His Court with the necessary rituals. She knows that over the years I have gradually slipped away from the faith in which I was so strictly brought up.

As I pack my clothes into the suitcase, I recall our early days in Paterson, New Jersey, where we lived for most of my adolescence while my father was alive and stationed in Brooklyn Yard in New York. At that time, our Catholic faith determined our family's views on most things, from clothing to the unmentioned subject of sex. Religion was the shield we had developed against the cold, foreign city. These days we have traded places in a couple of areas since she has gone home to make a new life for herself after my father's death. I chose to attend college in the United States and make a living as an English teacher and, lately, on the lecture circuit as a novelist and poet. But, though our lives are on the surface radically different, my mother and I have affected each other reciprocally over the past twenty years; she has managed to liberate herself from the rituals, mores, and traditions that "cramp" her style, while retaining her femininity and "Puertoricanness," while I struggle daily to consolidate my opposing cultural identities. In my adolescence, divided into my New Jersey years and my Georgia years, I received an education in the art of cultural compromise.

In Paterson in the 1960s I attended a public school in our neighborhood. Still predominantly white and Jewish, it was rated very well academically in a city where the educational system was in chaos, deteriorating rapidly as the best teachers moved on to suburban schools following the black and Puerto Rican migration into, and the white exodus from, the city proper. The Jewish community had too much at stake to make a fast retreat; many of the small businesses and apartment buildings in the city's core were owned by Jewish families of the

World War II generation. They had seen worse things happen than the influx of black and brown people that was scaring away the Italians and the Irish. But they too would gradually move their families out of the best apartments in their buildings and into houses in East Paterson, Fairlawn, and other places with *lawns.* That was how I saw the world then; either you lived without your square of grass, or you bought a house to go with it. But for most of my adolescence, I lived among the Jewish people of Paterson. We rented an apartment owned by the Milsteins, proprietors also of the deli on the bottom floor. I went to school with their children. My father took his business to the Jewish establishments, perhaps because these men symbolized "dignified survival" to him. He was obsessed with privacy and could not stand the personal turns conversations almost always took when two or more Puerto Ricans met casually over a store counter. The Jewish men talked too, but they concentrated on externals. They asked my father about his job, politics, his opinion on Vietnam, Lyndon Johnson. And my father, in his quiet voice, answered their questions knowledgeably. Sometimes before we entered a store — the cleaners or a shoe-repair shop — he would tell me to look for the blue-inked numbers on the owner's left forearm. I would stare at these numbers, now usually faded enough to look like veins in the wrong place. I would try to make them out. They were a telegram from the past, I later decided, informing the future of the deaths of millions. My father discussed the Holocaust with me in the same hushed tones my mother used to talk about God's Mysterious Ways. I could not reconcile both in my mind. This conflict eventually led to my first serious clash with my mother over irreconcilable differences between the "real world" and religious doctrine.

It had to do with the Virgin Birth.

And it had to do with my best friend and study partner, Ira Nathan, the acknowledged scientific genius at school. In junior high school it was almost a requirement to be "in love" with an older boy. I was an eighth grader and Ira was in the ninth grade that year, preparing to be sent away to some prep school in New

England. I chose him as my boyfriend (in the eyes of my classmates, if a girl spent time with a boy that meant they were "going together") because I needed tutoring in biology—one of his best subjects. I ended up having a crush on him after our first Saturday morning meeting at the library. Ira was my first exposure to the wonders of an analytical mind.

The problem was the subject. Biology is a dangerous topic for young teenagers who are themselves walking laboratories, experimenting with interesting combinations of chemicals every time they make a choice. In my basic biology class, we were looking at single-cell organisms under the microscope and watching them reproduce in slow-motion films in a darkened classroom. Though the process was as unexciting as watching a little kid blow bubbles, we were aroused by the concept itself. Ira's advanced class was dissecting fetal pigs. He brought me a photograph of his project, inner organs labeled neatly on the paper the picture had been glued to. My eyes refused to budge from the line drawn from "genitals" to a part of the pig to which it pertained. I felt a wave of heat rising from my chest to my scalp. Ira must have seen my discomfort, though I tried to keep my face behind the black curtain of my hair, but as the boy-scientist, he was relentless. He actually traced the line from label to pig with his pencil.

"All mammals reproduce sexually," he said in a teacherly monotone.

The librarian, far off on the other side of the room, looked up at us and frowned. Logically, it was not possible that she could have heard Ira's pronouncement, but I was convinced that the mention of sex enhanced the hearing capabilities of parents, teachers, and librarians by one hundred percent. I blushed more intensely and peeked through my hair at Ira.

He was holding the eraser of his pencil on the pig's blurry sexual parts and smiling at me. His features were distinctly Eastern European. I had recently seen the young singer Barbra Streisand on the Red Skelton show and had been amazed at how much similarity there was in their appearances. She could have been his sister. I was particularly attracted to the wide mouth and strong nose. No one that I knew in school thought that Ira was attractive, but his brains had long ago overshadowed his looks as his most impressive attribute. Like Ira, I was also a straight-A student and also considered odd because I was one of the few Puerto Ricans on the honor roll. So it didn't surprise anyone that Ira and I had drifted toward each other. Though I could not have articulated it then, Ira was seducing me with his No. 2 pencil and the laboratory photograph of his fetal pig. The following Saturday, Ira brought in his advanced biology book and showed me the transparencies of the human anatomy in full color that I was not meant to see for a couple more years. I was shocked. The cosmic jump between paramecium and the human body was almost too much for me to take in. These were the first grown people I had ever seen naked, and they revealed too much.

"Human sexual reproduction can only take place when the male's sperm is introduced into the female's womb and fertilization of the egg takes place," Ira stated flatly.

The book was open to the page labeled, "The Human Reproductive System." Feeling that my maturity was being tested, as well as my intelligence, I found my voice long enough to contradict Ira.

"There has been one exception to this, Ira." I was feeling a little smug about knowing something that Ira obviously did not.

"Judith, there are no exceptions in biology, only mutations, and adaptations through evolution." He was smiling in a superior way.

"The Virgin Mary had a baby without . . ." I couldn't say *having sex* in the same breath as the name of the Mother of God. I was totally unprepared for the explosion of laughter that followed my timid statement. Ira had crumpled in his chair and was laughing so hard that his thin shoulders shook. I could hear the librarian approaching. Feeling humiliated, I started to put my books together. Ira grabbed my arm.

"Wait, don't go." He was still giggling uncontrollably. "I'm sorry. Let's talk a little more. Wait, give me a chance to explain."

Reluctantly, I sat down again mainly because the librarian was already at our table, hands on hips, whispering angrily: "If you *children* cannot behave in this *study area*, I will have to ask you to leave." Ira and I both apologized, though she gave him a nasty look because his mouth was still stretched from ear to ear in a hysterical grin.

"Listen, listen. I'm sorry that I laughed like that. I know you're Catholic and you believe in the Virgin Birth" (he bit his lower lip trying to regain his composure), "but it's just not bio-logically possible to have a baby without" — he struggled for control — "losing your virginity."

I sank down on my hard chair. "Virginity." He had said an-other of the forbidden words. I glanced back at the librarian, who was keeping her eye on us. I was both offended and excited by Ira's blasphemy. How could he deny a doctrine that people had believed in for two thousand years? It was part of my prayers every night. My mother talked about La Virgen as if she were our most important relative.

Recovering from his fit of laughter, Ira kept his hand dis-creetly on my elbow as he explained in the seductive language of the scientific laboratory how babies were made and how it was impossible to violate certain natural laws.

"Unless God wills it," I argued feebly.

"There is no God," said Ira, and the last shred of my inno-cence fell away as I listened to his arguments backed up by ir-refutable scientific evidence.

Our meetings continued all that year, becoming more excit-ing with every chapter in his biology book. My grades improved dramatically, since one-celled organisms were no mystery to a student of advanced biology. Ira's warm, moist hand often brushed against mine under the table at the library, and walking home one bitter cold day, he asked me whether I would wear his Beta Club pin. I nodded, and when we stepped inside the hall-way of my building, where he removed the thick mittens that his mother had knitted, he pinned the blue enamel β to my collar. And to the hissing of the steam heaters, I received a serious kiss from Ira. We separated abruptly when we heard Mrs. Milstein's door open.

"Hello, Ira."

"Hello, Mrs. Milstein."

"And how is your mother? I haven't seen Fritzie all week. She's not sick, is she?"

"She's had a mild cold, Mrs. Milstein. But she is steadily improving." Ira's diction became extremely precise and formal when he was in the presence of adults. As an only child and a prodigy, he had to live up to very high standards.

"I'll call her today," Mrs. Milstein said, finally looking over at me. Her eyes fixed on the collar of my blouse, which was, I later saw in our hall mirror, sticking straight up with Ira's pin attached crookedly to the edge.

"Good-bye, Mrs. Milstein."

"Nice to see you, Ira."

Ira waved awkwardly to me as he left. Mrs. Milstein stood in the humid hallway of her building, watching me run up the stairs.

Our "romance" lasted only a week, long enough for Mrs. Milstein to call Ira's mother and for Mrs. Nathan to call my mother. I was subjected to a lecture on moral behavior by my mother, who, carried away by her anger and embarrassed that I had been seen kissing a boy (understood: a boy who was not even Catholic), had begun reciting a litany of metaphors for the loss of virtue.

"A cheap item," she said, trembling before me as I sat on the edge of my bed, facing her accusations, "a girl begins to look like one when she allows herself to be *handled* by men."

"Mother . . ." I wanted her to lower her voice so that my father, sitting at the kitchen table reading, would not hear. I had already promised her that I would confess my sin that Saturday and take communion with a sparkling clean soul. I had not been successful at keeping the sarcasm out of my voice. Her fury was fueled by her own bitter catalogue.

"A burden to her family . . ." She was rolling with her Spanish now; soon the Holy Mother would enter into the picture for good measure. "It's not as if I had not taught you better. Don't you know that those people do not have the example of the Holy Virgin Mary and her Son to follow and that is why they do things for the wrong reasons? Mrs. Nathan said she did not want her son messing around with you—not because of the wrongness of it—but because it would interfere with his studies!" She was yelling now. "She's afraid that he will"—she crossed herself at the horror of the thought—"make you pregnant!"

"We could say an angel came down and put a baby in my stomach, Mother." She had succeeded in dragging me into her field of hysteria.

"I do not want you associating any more than necessary with people who do not have God, do you hear me?"

"They have a god!" I was screaming now too, trying to get away from her. "They have an intelligent god who doesn't ask you to believe that a woman can get pregnant without having sex!"

"Nazi," I hissed. "I bet you'd like to send Ira and his family to a concentration camp!" At that time I thought that was the harshest thing I could have said to anyone. I was certain that I had sentenced my soul to eternal damnation the minute the words came out of my mouth, but I was so angry I wanted to hurt her.

Father walked into my room at that moment, looking shocked at the sight of the two of us entangled in mortal combat.

"Please, please." His voice sounded agonized. I ran to him, and he held me in his arms while I cried my heart out on his starched white shirt. My mother, also weeping quietly, tried to walk past us, but he pulled her into the circle. After a few moments, she put her trembling hand on my head.

"We are a family," my father said. "There is only just us against the world. Please, please . . ." But he did not follow the "please" with any suggestions as to what we could do to make things right in a world that was as confusing to my mother as it was to me.

I finished the eighth grade in Paterson, but Ira and I never got together to study again. I sent his Beta Club pin back to him through a mutual friend. Once in a while I saw him in the hall or the playground. But he seemed to be in the clouds, where he belonged. In the fall, I was enrolled at the Catholic high school, where everyone believed in the Virgin Birth, and I never had to take a test on the human reproductive system. It was a chapter that was not emphasized.

In 1968, my father retired from the navy and began looking for a better place for us to live. He decided to move us to Augusta, Georgia, where he had relatives who had settled after retiring from the army at Fort Gordon. They had convinced him that it was a healthier place to rear teenagers. For me, it was a shock to the senses, like moving from one planet to another. Paterson had concrete to walk on and gray skies, bitter winters, and a smorgasbord of an ethnic population; Georgia was red like Mars, and Augusta was green — exploding in colors in more gardens of azaleas and dogwood and magnolia trees, more vegetation than I imagined possible anywhere that was not tropical like Puerto Rico. People seemed to come in two basic colors: black and blond. And I could barely understand my teachers when they talked in a slowed-down version of English, like one of those old 78 rpm recordings played at 33. But I was placed in all advanced classes, and one of them was biology. This is where I got to see my first real fetal pig, which my assigned lab partner had chosen. She picked it up gingerly by the ends of the plastic bag in which it was stored: "Ain't he cute?" she asked. I nodded, nearly fainting from the overwhelming combination of the smell of formaldehyde and my sudden flashback to my brief but intense romance with Ira Nathan.

"What you want to call him?"

My partner unwrapped our specimen on the table, and I surprised myself by my instant recall of Ira's chart. I knew all the parts. In my mind's eye I saw the pencil lines, the labeled photograph. I had had an excellent teacher.

"Let's call him Ira."

"That's a funny name, but OK." My lab partner, a smart girl destined to become my mentor in things Southern, then gave me a conspiratorial wink and pulled out a little perfume atomizer from her purse. She sprayed Ira from snout to tail with it. I noticed this operation was taking place at other tables too. The teacher had conveniently left the room a few minutes before. I was once again stunned — almost literally knocked out by a fist of smell.

"What is it?"

"*Intimate*," my advanced biology partner replied smiling.

And by the time our instructor came back to the room, we were ready to delve into this mystery of muscle and bone; eager to discover the secrets that lie just beyond fear and a little past loathing; acknowledging the corruptibility of the flesh and our own fascination with the subject.

As I finish packing, the telephone rings and it's my mother. She is reminding me to be ready to visit relatives, to go to a dance with her, and, of course, to attend a couple of the services at the church. It is the feast of the Black Virgin, revered patron saint of our hometown in Puerto Rico. I agree to everything and find myself anticipating the eclectic itinerary. Why not allow Evolution and Eve, Biology and the Virgin Birth? Why not take a vacation from logic? I will not be away for too long; I will not let myself be tempted to remain in the sealed garden of blind faith; I'll stay just long enough to rest myself from the exhausting enterprise of leading the examined life.

VOODOO FAUST

Mary Hanford

 slumped into the broken wood seat in the African airport, shifting as splinters pierced my backside. Adolescent boys hovered around me clamoring to *gardez les bagages*. I waved them away; they drew back, then returned, like wasps. Flies circled a dead cat lying near the immigration counter. I covered my face with a scarf and slumped even further, pretending to sleep. After a year of teaching, I had requested a leave. Now I waited for a European plane to carry me to Chicago for medical care.

Neither the U.S. Embassy nurse nor the French doctors could rid me of my cough. Nor could they ease my pain in urination or the agony when someone thumped my kidney area. Habitually plump, I was now ten pounds underweight. Only a tonic prescribed by an African M.D. and four weeks of bedrest had helped me.

If those authorities had known my crushed spirits, they would have known why I fell sick—rejection by Ako, an African fon (local prince) and my program administrator. I loved Ako as I had loved no one else. I would have left everything to live with him. I even would have shared this brilliant man who read minds and who moved like a snake. He had been my guide, my protector, the one who acclimated me to Africa. He taught me many things: how to dodge the police and how to forge passports, when to use "medicine" on people and how to hear spirit guides. Later he taught me the soul travel that led me to "know" things and so avoid trouble.

I remembered the morning I returned from market to find my things stacked outside his door, a Muslim symbol of divorce. "How can you be divorced?" a neighbor asked. "You are not married."

"I was," I said. "He wasn't."

"They are all like that," another woman giggled.

He did take me back to my cubicle provided by the Ministry of Education. There I translated colonial documents from French to English, a two-year project that was funded by USAID.

Later I went through the motions of daily life and tried to remain calm. A teacher at the American School counseled me to stay friends. "You need a male in a country like this," she said.

Then the pains had started. They had continued until I had ended here in this decrepit waiting room, waiting for Swissair to fly me to a white doctor in a white room who would order for me white pills for an African ailment he never heard of. "Ju-ju would be better," I thought. African witchcraft accounted for most healings as well as for mischief, why not for me now? I didn't want to face the pale-skinned doctor with his white powders and his white coat, his white-clad nurse, his white bill. They wouldn't know that the red that swirled in my urine was blood wrung from my heart. Whites didn't think like that; white,

white, white, white . . . the word sounded in my mind like a curse.

"Racism in reverse," I thought. To Africans, white is the evil color, not black, as we think — white magic is ju-ju, not black magic — there was nothing I could do. My eyes stung from mascara that the tears dissolved into my pupils. I boarded the plane. With Swiss efficiency the stewardess led me, half-blinded, to my assigned seat. She asked whether I had lost a loved one. "Yes," I gulped.

The stewardess disappeared, then returned with a wet towel for my forehead, a glass of red wine, and some blood sausage with crackers.

As the plane took off, I curled into the seat. I felt defeated, as if all I attempted crumbled, as if I were the laughing stock of an unseen audience who pulled life's strings.

It isn't all bad to be defeated, I thought. At least I don't have to try to figure things out anymore. It's impossible, or if it is possible, I can't do it. Neither can anyone I know. The hot cloth and the wine made me drowsy; I mused about hometown U.S.A., neatly structured lives, houses, marriages, careers, people worrying about thunder thighs and animal rights. They were ridiculous. But at least they believed in order and control, that if worked for, justice could be achieved. I can't believe in it anymore, I thought. I've seen too much. I thought of the child who had died of measles in my arms when a vaccine was available twenty miles away. I thought of the fon's racism toward me and the excuse I heard everywhere that anything corrupt or evil in Africa was the result of white colonialism. Africa had the strength of complication, of a hybrid.

Even the missionaries in Africa seemed absurd, like Americans worrying over oat bran. In their attempts to evangelize with a simple gospel, they were trying to bail the ocean with a teaspoon. I had seen how years of being missionaries carved Africa into the preachers, not Christ into the Africans. Trying to change Africa, whether in religion or in language, was hopeless.

Maybe these efforts resulted in their myth of the Big White Bogey Man, seemingly helpful but really evil.

Christ — a baffling concept — tiered like a wedding cake, Father, Son, and Holy Ghost. I wished I knew more about it — sin, repentance, conversion, stuff like that. To Protestants snug in Calvin and a Midwestern winter, it made sense. To Catholics? I didn't know; in Africa they let polygamous wives take communion and go to confession. What they would confess, I couldn't fathom. . . . Africans didn't have sin. They sometimes believed in a colonial plot to destroy joy in living.

I wished I could do something about something, anything. My side ached and so did my neck. I pushed the button on my armrest, and the seat reclined.

In the lowered seat, I napped under the facecloth that I had draped the way I had done the scarf at the airport. I dreamed of a chicken that was having its feathers plucked while I looked on. "What are you going to do with the feathers?" I asked the plucker, whose back was the only thing I could see.

"Here, a bit of schnapps for you." The stewardess's voice startled me awake.

"Thanks."

Taking the schnapps forced me to remove the headcloth. I looked around. I had the center seat of a triple-seat row, so I could neither look out the window nor survey the aisle. There was no one in the aisle seat. In the window seat sat a large man gazing out the window. I guessed he was six four or five, but I couldn't really judge since he was sitting down. He was white and dumpy, like the Pillsbury Dough Boy. Rolls showed through his white shirt and a stomach spilled onto his white trousers. His pleasant expression as he studied the clouds could have been a travel advertisement. Something about his blandness gave me the creeps, as if that blandness masked . . . vacancy . . . a hole? As I rearranged skirt and magazines so as to drink the schnapps, he turned and said, "*Ça-va maintenant?*"

"Yes, thank you. I'm fine."

"Are you going to Zurich?" he continued in English.

"No, are you?"

"Yes, I am going to see my son. Where are you from?"

"Yaoundé, Cameroon."

"No, but so am I! And we have not met."

His smile was boyish, despite his middle age. He was gentle, but his eyes looked like those of foxes frozen in scrutiny. I felt fascinated. We began to chat in English.

Doughboy was the hotel manager of a swank hotel near Omnisport. I didn't understand his name when he said it or even when I read it on his card. He told me he was respected in the hotel in Yaoundé, but although the money was good, the job was not challenging. Since he had to support his son, he stayed there. Still, the money enabled him to return often to Switzerland to see his son and to visit his real home, Togo.

"Togo?" I asked. "I thought you were Swiss?"

"I am by birth, but physical birth means nothing. My father is in Togo."

"What is your father doing in Togo? Does he have a business there?" I asked, envisioning a Swiss watch shop in tropical Togo.

"Yes, you could call it a business," smiled the doughboy. "He is my spiritual father; I have studied Togolese voodoo with him for thirteen years. We lived in the bush, and he taught me everything."

"Oh," I said. My gut tensed; I was not used to this kind of talk from a white European. Did he know about Ako? No, he couldn't. I told myself not to be paranoid. "Your study is unusual for a Westerner."

"It is amazing how Europeans want to keep quiet the power available. They only want their microbes and surgical instruments recognized, like a business monopoly. I am convinced that the reason African spiritual knowledge is discredited is so that the world will not lose its Eurocentric bias. Like the church prohibited the works of Galileo."

"What can voodoo do for you, or for me?" I thought he was right but felt uneasy, like the first time I walked through an African market at night.

"First, I want to say that you need to have your neck looked at when you return to the United States. It has damaged vertebrae and will cause you much pain, perhaps nerve damage, if it is not attended to."

He had not touched or even looked at my neck, which was covered by my blouse's ruffles.

"Don't be afraid," the man said. "I know because you are cold in the neck area. I noticed it when you sat down. It was not your head that concerned me, but that chill in the neck. I didn't say anything because we were not talking. I also hesitated, for such a condition comes with /age, and it's not a gallant thing to tell a lady."

Then I did feel a chill. Doughboy's affability reminded me of those incandescent bulbs whose light produces no warmth. "I'm going to the United States for medical care, but it's not about my neck," I said.

"You will find it is as I say. I just wanted to tell you, so you don't waste your trip," smiled the man. He seemed to leer slightly, like a monk who'd had a nun the night before. His white clothes waved like robes.

"You are very kind. Tell me about your 'father.'"

"He tutored me in the Togolese bush. I was in Togo on a mission for the Swiss. Now I communicate with him from Yaoundé, in a special room in the hotel."

"Do you have a fax machine there?"

He smiled. "No, Madame. We communicate here," he pointed to his head.

"Telepathically?"

"*Bien sûr*," he smiled again. "Since I have become a master, we communicate often. If there is a problem and I cannot solve it with my god, I do something, and *voilà*! there is my father. He tells me what to do."

"Yes, I know how that works." I felt on familiar territory, as I knew the fon talked often with the village shaman.

"Let me give you an example. In 1978 we had a fellow in the hotel in Lomé who had epileptic seizures. He was French, and

all the medicine from Paris had not controlled it. He would
weep after an episode, for he knew that sooner or later these
fits would cost him his job. Word would get around. You know
how it is."

"Yes," I said.

"I took him into the forest to my father. We gathered the others and put Jean in the middle. I cannot explain with my English what we did. But afterwards, he was cured. He is still fine.
That's what Europe will not accept."

"What else can you do with it besides cure people; can you
curse them? That's what I've always heard about voodoo."

"*Bien sûr.* But I wear white to signal to those who know
about us that I am harmless. I practice only white magic, never
black. Those who are familiar with us will know which side I
am on." He smiled, a Santa Claus of magic.

"It takes training and work, like anything else. I depend heavily on my god; he gives me power. I can work my will with it. In
a scattered and predatory world, I can control my destiny."

"How do you get what you want?" I asked, inexplicably
remembering the Africans' distrust of white.

"Ah, *ma petite*" — for the first time speaking familiarly — "it
would take more time than we have for me to tell you."

"What if I want something that involves someone else? A marriage, for example; can I make another person marry?" I asked.

"Yes, but it takes a lot of energy. You must be very strong. To
materialize a marriage is a lot of work, but it can be done.
It's whether you want to put in the effort and whether you have
the strength to endure it. There was a man in Yaoundé who
wanted to marry a very 'contrary' woman. He asked me for
help. We had to get pictures of him and of her, but eventually
the marriage was accomplished. First, she slowly dropped her
other lovers; then they lived together. Now they are married. But
it takes a lot of energy to bring another person to you. There is
nothing, actually, you cannot have if you are willing to learn."

"I am willing," I heard myself say, "I am tired of being pushed
around by God knows what."

"You use a word with a big letter; perhaps you should think about what would do you the most good, not follow sheeplike the bleatings of religion."

Doughboy giggled; his rolls of flesh bounced as if in a jig. "I am close to my god; he gives me power. I sleep with him every night. If you are serious, you must destroy your handbag."

I glanced at my python-skin purse lying under our two seats. "My purse?"

"My god is the python. He sleeps with me. Father and I are in close communication through the python. From it, I get strength. Your god would be different."

"Oh." I remembered what the fon had taught me: that there are levels of spiritual reality as there are strata of earth. He had likened it to a geologist's labeling different eras by the various compositions of rocks.

A voice whined in four languages over the loudspeaker. We buckled our seatbelts. In ten minutes, we were in Zurich.

"If you truly want to learn, I will help you," said the man. He reached into a pocket on his white jacket and pulled out his wallet. The wallet was not made of skin of any sort. I couldn't tell what it was made of. He pulled out a business card and handed it to me. "This is my hotel's address and phone number in Yaoundé. Look for me there. I like you. I will help you. Your life will change."

"Thank you."

He helped me get my carry-all out of the overhead compartment; we left the plane together. At a Swissair ticket counter, he bent over and kissed me on the neck. "Destroy that purse before you call." His breath smelled like candy, with a slight acrid undertone — as if someone had added too much of some kind of extract.

I turned toward the duty-free shop. I didn't look to see where he was going but guessed it was to get his luggage. I had a craving for chocolate, Swiss chocolate. At the shop, I bought a box of fifty tiny bars for eleven American dollars. Then I sat to await the plane to Chicago. I finished the chocolates in thirty minutes.

They tasted like Doughboy's breath smelled. Scraps of gold foil lay about my feet.

I took out the doughboy's card from my pocket and then stuffed it in my wallet. "Opportunity knocks," I thought. "Maybe, maybe, maybe — I can stop being pushed around, can push instead of being pushed." I remembered a youth group minister's warning about magic when I was in high school. He just toed a party line, I thought. He wouldn't know a voodoo master if he tripped over one. Without picking up the foil, I sauntered to the newsstand and bought a copy of French-language *Elle*.

In Chicago, I learned I had a lung fungus. X-rays showed a kidney infection and an enlarged ovary. They also showed bone damage: damaged neck vertebrae.

"I know," I said to the doctor.

"How did you know? Did you feel it?"

"Sort of."

"Well, physical therapy may help, but there's no way to restore the damage," the doctor went on.

"Yes, there is."

The doctor looked at me, "How?"

"Mend a broken heart!" I cried. Suddenly, I felt mortified. Emotional declarations were acceptable in Yaoundé, but not Chicago. Just as suddenly, I felt guilty. "Sorry, don't mean to be a pain." I turned and hurried out, ashamed, but enraged at the doctor's clinical approach. This so-called expert was like a man with cataracts trying to read a contract. He thought he understood, but missed the fine print. I hated him and every obtuse Westerner.

As the skyscraper's revolving door turned me onto the street, I saw a wooden sign with a painted arrow pointing to the left. It said, "Our Lady of Perpetual Hope Church. Masses said in English and Spanish."

I turned left and headed for the church. I was neither Latin nor Catholic; I was Anglo-American and Nothing. But I wanted the comfort of an old building and an old language.

It was dank inside the church. Nothing was going on. Except for two or three children who wandered in and out, there was no one at all in the dark sanctuary. I wondered whether I should walk up to the altar, sit down, kneel. . . .

"May I help you? You look lost," someone said.

I turned to see a young black man in a priest's cassock. Except for his potbelly and eyeglasses, he looked uncomfortably like my fon. Maybe it was his priest's cap; it looked like a fon's hat.

"I thought this was a Spanish church," I said.

"So a black priest can't serve in a bicultural church?" he asked, his face rippling into smiles.

Whether it was because he was black and kindly or because I was distraught, I blurted, "I don't know anything about Catholics, but I know you do confession; will you listen?" Without waiting for an answer, I told of my soured love affair, the man on the airplane, and the medical opinion. When I finished, we were both leaning against a pew. The priest's interested expression was replaced by an anxious one.

"Come with me," he said.

We went into a small office where he sat down behind a scuffed desk with a gold-colored woodcarving of Mary on it. "I don't know what I'm supposed to do in this situation. Certainly you sinned, but you are not a Catholic, so I can't absolve you."

"What sin?" I asked.

His face drooped, suddenly tired. "Sexual intercourse outside of marriage."

"Oh."

"But that's not the worst sin, and I can't be bothered with bureaucratic questions about what to do with a non-Catholic's confession. But stay away from anyone who practices black magic!"

"It's not black magic. It's voodoo. There's a difference."

"What is it?"

"There are levels of spirituality, and many powers that can be tapped into and used. Some people use the powers for good, not ill; voodoo can be either black magic or white magic," I said.

"Don't be naive," he snapped. "Your soul is at stake."

"Soul?" I said. "That means my fon was wrong too. He soul travels."

"You keep your soul right in your body, do you understand? Magic is wrong, no matter what color you call it, and dangerous! It's manipulating the universe to get one's own way, instead of submitting to Almighty God." The priest's furrowed black face looked like newly tilled soil.

A recording of church bells began to chime. The priest started. "Time for noon mass. I must get vested. I don't know what more to tell you," he said, running from the office and leaving the door ajar. But he wasn't four feet out of the office before he turned around, "Yes, I do know. Remember, you can always call on God for help!"

Again, my stomach clenched in anger. Didn't he know I was tired of calling for help? And how could he just run out on me that way? Some ritual was more important than I. Only the priest's caring manner and something homey about the dilapidated church, like a much-used but loved kitchen, kept me from spitting on it.

As I walked to the train station, I reflected. The only difference I could see between these Catholics and voodoo was this submitting to, instead of controlling of, one's destiny. Baloney, I thought. As I boarded Amtrak's Silver Eagle, I starting thinking about my hometown.

I found that much had changed there. Tenants had wrecked my house, and my time overseas had worsened my job prospects. There was a gap between me and my friends, not just a time-made void, but one that resulted from the radically different culture that I had experienced. I didn't know where I belonged. America's plenty mesmerized me. I could not shake a fascination with people's pantries or choose from a restaurant menu without help. Television commercials for fancy pet food angered me, and that anger embarrassed my friends. The United States seemed cold, lonely, and frantic. I felt relief when I boarded an Air France flight to return to Cameroon. In my purse, I carried six bottles of antibiotics.

At "home," things progressed normally, that is, not at all. I improved physically, but not much. I thought about Dough-boy's offer, but his card had evidently fallen out of my wallet. I woke at 5:00 A.M. to the call of the minaret for prayer, napped during the afternoon heat, and caught the maid pilfering grocery money. Friends visited and gave parties. Nothing "happened." It was triumph enough to survive, particularly during the dry season. Those who could went to the mountains to escape the heat.

I did not want to see the fon. In the United States, I had fancied that I was now sick of him, the way I surfeited on too much chocolate. He had been there waiting for me at 2:00 A.M. when my plane landed. Following my friend Margaret's advice to "stay friends," I had been polite. Now he showed up periodically to ask about my health or on some other excuse. I couldn't tell whether he was doing what he thought was his duty or whether a flame remained. Margaret's pragmatic advice cost me. I was in anguish whenever he was around. I could not believe it was over.

This self-deception led me into the next delusion. I had a chance to go to the mountains, where the evenings were cool and fresh. My job required translating archives in the Northwest province. I had a place to stay; the U.S. government would provide a vehicle. I was relating this to Ako in an offhand manner when he said, "I will take you. The heat is too much for you here. The roads are treacherous, and there are police blocks. I will visit my family up North."

Jubilantly, I told Margaret when she dropped in that night to bring me bootlegged commissary food. "He still cares! I know it; he's driving me eight hours to the North."

"Don't go," said Margaret, sorting the food into refrigerated and nonrefrigerated items. "Don't be shut up with him all that time."

"Why not?"

Margaret drummed her fingers on the countertop and stared out the kitchen window, as if she saw something far off. "What if you find out—oh, I don't know, really. I just don't think it's a good idea. What if, what if he criticizes you all that time, or ignores you?"

Margaret was wrong. Her advice to keep Ako as a friend had already hurt me. I didn't want this advice to cost me an opportunity. "I'm going," I said.

"Well, I wouldn't go there," said Margaret, wiping the counter with a rag. "But I will go home; I want to miss traffic. You can write me a check later." Margaret swept out the door, calling for her driver.

Margaret was pragmatic to the point of deadliness. Her practicality choked romance. It was like her to look a gift horse in the mouth. As I prepared for bed, for the first time in a year I felt gratitude. I even tried to thank God that night. I began the prayer I had learned as a child, "Now I lay me down to sleep . . . ," but couldn't remember the rest.

When Ako picked me up, I saw we had another passenger. "I'm giving cousin Linus a lift. He lives an hour before the Northwest Province," said Ako. To hide my disappointment, I ducked my head so fast that my ivory barrette fell from my hair. The drive was hot the first few hours. We wound through the garbage-strewn streets of Yaoundé, and then through steamy jungle, before we reached the road to the mountains. I sat in the back, chewing my hair and feeling abandoned. There was no way Ako and I could talk. In the front seats, the two men talked politics in French. "A man in Douala was arrested by the secret police and was never heard from again," said the cousin.

"What happened to his car?" asked Ako.

I didn't care about all this. As the scenery changed from twisted emerald jungle to wheat-colored savannahs to slate-colored mountains, I plotted. Once we dropped the cousin off, we would have an hour together; maybe then I could get something out of Ako. It didn't make sense that he would go all this way for my sake if he didn't care.

"Your friend is very pretty," the cousin said to Ako.

"*Oui, oui,*" Ako answered, assuming a stony expression.

I spent the drive looking out the window and rehearsing what I was going to say to Ako when we were finally alone. I wanted to get him in a position where he would have to talk straight.

"After we drop Linus in Baufassom, let's stop and have a drink at the Picon Rouge before going on. You must be tired of driving, and I am thirsty," I suggested.

"I am never tired," said Ako.

Just before sunset, we sat on the balcony of the Picon Rouge Café. The Picon Rouge was popular because of its informal, accepting atmosphere. I thought of the Chicago church as Ako and I took seats at a tiny table on the balcony near the stairs. The Picon Rouge's upstairs balcony circled the whole building. There Westerners and Africans mingled easily, eating, drinking, watching the streetlife of the province's capital and the mountains change color as day waned.

Ako ordered goat pepper stew. I had only a pamplemousse. We didn't say anything. I peered at Ako over my straw. His face, so focused on the stew, reminded me of the faces of presidents carved in the South Dakota hills. Now that my chance had come, my nerve failed. I didn't know what to say, how to begin. What could I say? "Why don't you love me? You MUST love me, you MUST because you drove me here, you MUST because I want you to. . . ." My stomach churned, and I felt an explosion about to happen in my gut. Maybe the pamplemousse had been made with bad water. "I need to go to the bathroom," I said. "Will you excuse me?"

"Do you know where it is?"

"No."

Ako snapped his fingers. The waiter appeared. They whispered; the waiter disappeared. Shortly, a teenager appeared and beckoned to me, then led me to the backyard where there was a tiny shed. She unlocked the door to the shed and motioned for me to go in. Inside was a hole in the earth floor and some palm leaves beside the hole. "I can't even shit without his help!" I thought and squatted over the hole.

But instead of an explosion, nothing happened. I was now knotted up. "My emotions always show in my gut," I admitted. To relax I started to daydream. I began to remember pieces of a dream I'd had the night before. In the dream Ako and I were going to a party. We arrived, but there was no one there. Then a small, slim African girl appeared. Her looks were vague, but I knew she was young. Ako motioned for me to sit down, which I did. He took my purse, then left as if to secure it. But instead he handed my purse to the girl, whom he bent down and kissed. A knowing gripped me. "Ako has a girlfriend! I know it; I dreamed it! I know he does! That's why he's being so nice to me, let me down easy — he knows I still love him. Africans dream things all the time, why not me?"

As I sat back down across from Ako, my stomach churned.

"Are you all right? You took a while, and you look pale," said Ako.

"You have a girlfriend."

"What makes you think that?"

"Well, do you?"

"Nonsense. You are hysterical as usual. How could I accept that position in the United States you've promoted for me, if I have ties here?"

"You have a girlfriend."

"In your usual screwball fashion, you are making excuses for something. There is something unwholesome about you. Why would I bring you all the way up here on the weekend if I had someone? How do you know I have a 'girlfriend,' as you put it?" asked Ako.

"I dreamed it. And you know I know, because YOU taught me with your soul-travel stuff how to get in tune, how to dream, how to listen to dreams . . . how to *know*!"

Ako was quiet. He put his palms together along with his fingers, as if to play, "Here's the church, here's the steeple." Then he tilted his chair back against the railing. He seemed to be thinking something over. I guessed he was going to tell me that my white colonial mentality had betrayed me and that he would never speak to me again. But still I kept on.

"How could you do this — bring me up here, keep me dangling — sending me all those mixed messages. Even when we shared the same bed, you were not this helpful!"

"She is here," said Ako, suddenly jerking himself and his chair upright.

"What? Who?"

"About one hour's drive north of where I will drop you. I was going to ask for the car to visit my family, then bring it back to you in the morning. It is not that I don't care for you, but something that cannot work should not be invested in. What do you think would happen. I, a fon, go live with you in racist United States?!"

"You're doing it again! The mixed message. 'Where there's a will, there's a way' we always say." I tore away from the table and ran down the rickety stairs to the main floor of the Picon Rouge. I ran back into the yard and behind the shed, so customers who had seen me run out could not stare.

Behind the shed I sobbed, "It's no use, no use. He taught me, and now I *know* things. What can I do? Inside, inside . . ." I fumbled in my purse, looking for money. I would demand the keys and drive the rest of the way myself. I could talk my way through roadblocks. Hell with him.

I couldn't find enough change, but some was underneath the wads of paper that always ended up in my purse. I grabbed out a fistful: napkins, copies of passport and health card, various business cards. One of the business cards leapt out at me: " 'Hotel Yaoundé: Gérald Jean Malfeau,' the voodoo man! Here it is! He said he'd help me. He said he could do a marriage. He said he could."

I walked back to the restaurant and asked whether there was a phone. I put in all my coins to cover long distance, then dialed the number on the business card. "Hotel Yaoundé," a cross female voice sounded through static.

It was a miracle there was a phone. It was a miracle it worked! Nothing, particularly phones, worked in Cameroon. It was a miracle I had dialed the right number!

I yelled into the receiver, "*Bon soir. M. Malfeau est là?*"

"*Un moment, Madame,*" the voice said.

"He's there. If I can just talk to him, make an appointment. God help me!"

Then the phone went dead.

I couldn't believe it! "Madame! Madame!" I screamed, trying to get the operator back. "*Au secours!*"

"It is not working," said the bartender.

"I know. I know the damn thing's not working. Make it work!"

"It is you who have made it work," he said. "That phone is out of order."

"What?"

"It worked when first put in last year, but that's all," said the bartender, wiping the bar with a cloth. "You are lucky you got a tone."

"No, no," I said. "I can't do anything; nothing works!"

"You must have magic in you, ju-ju, to connect dead phone."

"Not enough, not enough," I slumped against the bar.

"Get stronger magic."

"I'm trying, don't you understand?" The way a drowning victim's life passes before him, I recalled all Ako had taught me. If I could get through to Doughboy, if I could surpass him in "knowledge," Ako would be hoist on his own petard. Or would he? Would I? After all, the man who taught me all this had betrayed me.

I fumbled frantically with the receiver. Nothing happened. I pounded the phone, my gut again rumbling.

"It doesn't want to connect with you," said the bartender.

"It's not because I'm not trying, so help me God!" I clutched the phone as if it were a person.

The Chicago priest's kind face swam in my memory alongside Ako's granite expression. They were the same color, but not the same. And Doughboy? Maybe Doughboy was HIM, the GREAT WHITE BOGEYMAN, toying with me—only appearing to help. What good would any more "knowledge" do me? White and black skins—sins—magic; I was muddled. Something important but elusive was floating by, but I was too tired to grasp it.

I wanted to rest. I wanted to lie down in one of the Chicago church's friendly pews and be rocked by the concerned, scolding priest.

"Call on biggest God," the bartender said, looking at me standing by the dangling receiver.

"Maybe I just did," I said, wondering whether I was only relying on my own culture's god the way I would a teddy bear, the way I would that priest if he were here.

"Then give up," said the bartender pragmatically.

"Okay," I said, sitting down on a barstool. I ordered coffee, then stared at Doughboy's card. By the time the coffee arrived, I had shredded it into an emptied glass. When I went back to Ako's table, before he could speak, I demanded the car keys. It took me only five hours to drive myself home.

EXTENUATING CIRCUMSTANCES

Lauren B. Smith

 start this piece of writing on a trip to Paris where, despite the huge American presence, I am a stranger. I know I am a stranger because of the way people look at me — curiously, knowingly, and often as if I were a little crazy — especially when I speak. I speak tentatively anyway, as if I am putting my feet down on unfamiliar ground, touching with my toes first, then with the ball of my foot, feeling for loose stones or pointed rocks, then finally transferring all my weight. In Paris, as in any big city, I suppose, people are not very patient with this process. People aren't always patient with me in English. In French, it is just that much worse.

"How much to go to Luxembourg Garden," I ask slowly in French, "if I [*pause*] transfer [*pause*] at l'Hôtel de Ville?"

"Treize francs," says the bus driver, looking at me critically. "Treize" is thirteen, two dollars and sixty cents, a lot for a short bus ride, so I think he's saying three, "troi," sixty cents, much more reasonable.

"Treize!" says the bus driver exasperatedly. There are people behind me. I give him a twenty, take the change, and sit down. When my heart stops beating, I venture timidly, again in French, to the woman beside me, "Can I return with this?"

"Unfortunately, no," she says, smiling. She is much older than I am, maybe seventy-five, and for some reason older people are more patient with me. I smile back.

Hassimi is always patient with my French. He is, in fact, appreciative. The day I told him I spoke French — a little — he almost drove off the road with enthusiasm. Since then, he has maintained that my French is good, fine, wonderful, long after he could possibly have perceived it necessary to flatter me.

He is not just patient with me, though. If he'd been on the bus, he would have been patient with the bus driver, too, no matter how impatient the bus driver was with us.

"Well," he would begin with a musical, drawn-out *e-l-l* that always gives the following thought a certain dramatic emphasis, "he probably feels a lot of pressure, don't take it personally." Or "maybe he's just tired." Or something else about not getting needlessly upset, about not "making my life difficult," which is precisely what he says I always do.

On the other hand, he might attribute the driver's ill temper to his shortness. Being six-foot-nine and exceedingly mild-mannered, Hassimi attributes all sorts of quirks in character — especially bossiness, loudness, or overassertion of any sort — to shortness of stature.

My wonderful best friend J, for example, is petite, and she can, coincidentally, be a little bossy. I explained the early part of my friendship with J to Hassimi one day. We got along perfectly, I told him, because she sweetly led me around and I happily followed. "*Zeess,*" he pronounced (he has a French-African accent), "*izz because she izz short.*"

"What?" I said, a bit stunned. This was the first time I'd heard his analysis of the behavior of short people, and I certainly didn't expect to hear anything of the sort applied to my friend — who invariably manages to command respect in the world despite her mere sixty-three or so inches.

"Short people need to be heard," he told me. "They don't want to be forgotten."

This was something I didn't know how to respond to, so I just sat back and relished the prospect of explaining to J the source of her occasional bossiness.

Hassimi's pronouncement about short people does not at all mean that he doesn't like my friend J. Actually, he thinks she is quite wonderful. He calls her, asks about her, works hard to make time whenever she is in town. In fact, his explanation of J's bossiness does not even amount to a criticism of character and definitely not to a physical critique. J's shortness, rather, is an extenuating circumstance. It is a reason, if she should ever prove irritable or demanding, for us not to judge her too harshly. It is a fact of life, the smallest of natural disasters, something to be accepted and chuckled over.

The most intentionally mean I can remember having been to Hassimi was last fall. He had been working late in the laboratory every night for five or six nights in a row. What's more, he'd come back looking as he sometimes does — dishevelled, dusty, tired. He'd sit at the couch and stare at nothing if I was not directing conversation to him. Even then, he'd begin to lose track, make leaving movements midsentence. I had the sense that, if I wanted him to stay more than ten minutes, I couldn't even pause, I had to keep talking.

He hadn't come when I'd expected him to, anyway, and this happened all the time that fall; it still happens now. "I'll be there around nine-thirty," he would say, and when nine-thirty came, I'd sit under the picture window in the living room reading and occasionally looking out at the quiet street below. The house I lived in was up on a hill, and I could see parts of the city and university along the banks of the river that ran a block or so below. I'd look through my own reflection in the window at the lights and wonder where he was. Sometimes, the lab he was working in had a phone and sometimes it didn't. In any case, I got tired of calling him. I'd get someone rude or tired — or another inaccurate time.

Sometimes, it would click past eleven, past eleven-thirty. My own reflection got brighter as the night got darker — 'til I found myself looking at myself, finally, looking out.

On the night in question, I could see myself clearly in the living room window. There was a steeliness around the mouth I saw there, a bitterness I hate. My jaw was clenched, two deep lines chiseled at the corners. It was a mouth I remember from the days before my mother divorced, a mouth that would not unclose itself easily.

Finally, Hassimi's car scraped in at the driveway. I could see the print of his shirt coming up the front walk, and I went to open the door for him. As I expected, he looked wrinkled, dusty, as if he'd pulled himself out of storage somewhere, or as if he'd managed to retain some of the dust of Burkina Faso just under his skin.

I was mad at him for being late. I was mad at him for being tired. I was mad at him for being wrinkled and linty, not the cheerful and good-looking man of our first summer together. I was too mad to say how I was feeling, and perhaps it would have done no good anyway. Instead, we carried on a conversation — exhausted and mundane on his side, terse and ironic on mine. He seemed to be sliding away from me, getting smaller and smaller, as if I were looking at him through the wrong end of a telescope.

When he got up to leave, he said as always, "I love you." He smiled exhaustedly.

I folded my arms and with a thrill of pleasure told him, "I don't know if I love you anymore." There was a moment of triumph and then the man in front of me again. Two long frowns traced the curve of his forehead. The shadows of fatigue seemed to have deepened and spilled down. The muscles in his cheeks, slack. His mouth a surprised O, a Y of sadness between his eyes.

It was, of course, a lie; and what do you do to repair something as intentionally mean as that?

I called him later, but I'd been long forgiven: *people do things like that sometimes, my schedule is hard on you, you didn't mean it, it's just because you love me.* Of course, he was right. His schedule is very hard on me, and I do love him; but I didn't expect to be so easily pardoned. Actually, it was less forgiveness than a certain allowance, a margin of error, a place within which to move and think and react without diagnosis or confession. I was relieved, and it was a relief that extended out past our argument, even past our relationship itself. I am not a woman who loves too much. I do not have a Cinderella complex. I am not just like my bitter Aunt So and So.

He was late, and I was angry and disappointed. That's all.

Or maybe that isn't all. From a certain, rather persuasive, way of looking at it, a pattern has developed between us. He is the one who is always busy, always late, and I am the one who is mad and waiting. Even when I am the one who finds myself busy or behind schedule, things have an infuriating way of reversing themselves. If I show up twenty minutes late, he has received an important long-distance phone call by the time I arrive. If I am busy all day, he is busy all night.

I showed up fifteen minutes late for a picnic one day, for example. He was busy, so I had made a little supper myself and, waiting for the boiled eggs to cool, ended up arriving outside his lab at 5:15 instead of 5:00 as planned. I waited fifteen minutes. Because the prevailing ideology of the chemistry building holds that graduate students don't have the right to a private life, I am always a little afraid that my presence at his lab will cause Hassimi professional problems and am reluctant to go there. The chemistry building is huge, furthermore, and I have no way of knowing exactly where in it he is at any given moment. I went to find a phone and, by the time I got back, he'd already been to the car and returned to the huge labyrinth of the chemistry building. I waited for fifteen more minutes. When I finally went to the lab, both apprehensive and furious that he had not just waited for me at the car, Hassimi came to the door in his lab coat.

"Where the hell have you been?" I hissed.

"I was ready at five o'clock," he said. His forehead was wrinkled with worry and surprise.

His surprise itself infuriated me. I could hardly even think of anything to say.

"So you just put your lab coat on and go back to the lab?" My head was a giant, tense muscle, and I was pushing the words through my teeth. This picnic was the first fun thing we had planned together in weeks; and there was no way we would get our afternoon back now. Even if we did still go on our picnic, there was a fight ahead—between the two of us probably, between me and my disappointment most certainly. I thought, "He does not care about our time together, and I don't understand why he pretends to."

An explanation followed: He was ready; he didn't know where I was; his professor asked him to do something; I hadn't left a message; he thought I would come to the laboratory. Finally, could I please wait for him? Thirty minutes? I was too mad to do anything else anyway, so I waited—for forty-five minutes—or an hour.

When he finally did show up, it was almost two hours later than the time we'd originally scheduled. He looked penitent, wary, but also a little bewildered. I don't think he entirely understood why I was mad, but at that point I didn't care if he understood or not.

The thing I realized a couple of one-way fights later (Hassimi rarely gets angry) is that he really *didn't* understand why I was mad. What I heard and still hear as excuses, he understood as explanations. We didn't leave for our picnic until almost seven o'clock because of a series of circumstances unique to that moment in the universe, circumstances as unavoidable as they were unimportant. Once these circumstances were explained to me, he fully expected, things would be set right — no matter what time it was. When I was still mad, he repeated the circumstances to me like a chant, as if I had simply been unable to understand him. In fact, he listed these circumstances with a certain confidence, as if they could set back the clock or interrupt the pattern that had set in. It doesn't matter that we had planned three different times to see *Malcolm X* and never went. It does not matter that we had been talking about this picnic for two weeks.

It is not, I sometimes think, the picnic that is important to Hassimi at all. It is, rather, the intention to go on one that counts.

Hassimi's tendency to see every case as a discrete thing, an event unconnected to others, has its shortcomings. On a more serious, abstract level, we can know about and work on various social problems — things like xenophobia or sexism — only by pointing out social patterns that might not be strictly obvious or that people might prefer to deny. If, for example, we think of spouse abuse only in terms of the individual cases within which it occurs, we have no way of estimating the scope of the problem and no way of intervening. On a smaller scale, the same thing is also true of a relationship. You know what the problems are by looking at the patterns that develop.

On the other hand, a perfectly healthy society, if such a thing could be said to exist, would also function according to certain patterns. And we cannot always be sure of the meanings of those patterns we do find.

For example, on the day of the ill-fated picnic, I laid our relationship open for him as if it were a frog on the dissecting table. With teary-eyed confidence I pointed out its various parts and pathologies. The heart of the matter, I told him, was this: For him, I was part of the private, feminine sphere. However important he might say I was to him, however important I might actually be, I would always take a backseat to anything public, anything work-oriented, anything masculine. I am a woman, and therefore I am expected to wait. My feelings are of secondary importance, as are my plans or anything he might spend time doing that would make our relationship stronger.

"Wow!" he said. We were in the car on our way to Kent Park, and we were still en route when I had finished my delivery. We were well out of the city limits, driving by a field with horses, a crop of corn, a big white box of a house with small neat windows and no shutters.

"Why didn't you tell me you were thinking this way?" and then later, "Do you think I am crazy? Do you think I wouldn't rather be on a picnic with you than working in my lab? Do you think I wouldn't rather be making love, having a nice dinner, going dancing, having a talk with friends, going to hear some music?" Then he set off on the normal explanation: what had happened, what had been impossible.

It was not much different than any number of other discussions we have had, except perhaps in pitch. There was one difference, though.

I had expressed, this time, what was probably my biggest fear about our relationship, about him. It goes something like this: He has told me that he wants to get married, that he wants to have kids, a family, a home. I have never assumed that such things were coming my way, or even that I wanted them; but I have been relaxing into the future imperfect of these possibilities, trying them on in my imagination. What I fear is that after all the work I have done to reimagine my own life's possibilities, resisting the pull of the traditional script, I will be lured into just such a script by someone who wants the fantasy of a family more than he wants the real thing, who does not value the world traditionally occupied by women, who does not value women, who does not value me. It is not an unreasonable fear. I see women all around me who have been abandoned, emotionally or otherwise, by men who have found that the family they brought into this world interfered with their plans or desires, that the family they had was messier and more demanding than the family they had imagined.

I suspected Hassimi's lateness and frequent emotional un-availability to be evidence that he did not really value me or the domestic/feminine world. I suspected this despite the way he treats me when he is around; despite the way he treats my friends and family; the number of times he calls me on the tele-phone; the number of times he has mown my lawn and done my laundry, even washing some of it by hand; the way he shares his apartment and his car, which I have come to treat as if they were my own.

His reaction to my accusation, though, was not what I had expected. He did not belittle me for this idea or tell me I was overreacting or treat me like a corrosive material. "Do you think I am crazy?" he said, proceeding to list the things he could be doing if he were not in the lab — wistfully — and I suppose that was the key. The wistfulness did it. At least, it interrupted the straight path of my interpretation. It was like a bell ringing off in the distance, barely audible, when I had thought myself to be at sea. It was unsettling, coming to me through a fog of misun-derstanding. What could a bell signify, after all? Rocks? Land? Another ship? Things were not as I had thought they were. I could be looking at the wrong map. I could be in dangerous water or closer to home than I had thought.

In an earlier draft of this essay, I would arrive at this moment of confusion and explain it solely in terms of my own experi-ence. I wanted to describe the unsettling of my own certainties, to construct my own alternative to the story I had been telling myself. In order to do this, I had described Hassimi's life briefly, piecing together the fragments I already knew; and I had written this story in my own voice so that the writing would be consis-tent. Such consistency, however, such single-voicedness, began to seem too easy to me. It did not reflect the complication of what was at stake, the net of feelings and histories to be sorted out. I am an American woman struggling to speak, to matter, to have my contributions acknowledged and appreciated; but

Hassimi is an African man, and he is struggling, too. I decided to interview him, to ask him to tell his story in his own voice. Here are pieces of what he told me:

I came from a big family. My father used to have three wives, and right now I have one brother, one sister, four half-sisters and another half-brother. My parents didn't go to school, and they didn't speak French. In fact, my father died when I was less than a year old. My mother raised me alone, and I went to school without any knowledge of French. I went to school where no student could speak his native language, and I had to either shut up in class or find a way to see what the other students were doing. I had to imitate them. Honestly, I don't know today — if you asked me — how I passed the first or second grade; but I remember when I was in third grade, I was sitting under the trees while most of my friends were playing soccer and other games. I was reading my book, studying hard. Nobody was there to help me.

My mother didn't even know what to expect from school. Every month we had exams, so sometimes, after I learned French, I was the first in the class or the second. When I talked to my mother, she didn't know what I was talking about. I said, "Mum, I passed all the other students. I am number one." She said, "Oh. Good."

My mother sold doughnuts and cookies and peanuts in the farmer's market. She didn't have anything, but I never starved. Her house was not good. The roof was made with mud, and when it rained hard, the roof leaked. Sometimes when I slept, I would wake up and find mud on my head. Sometimes I was deep asleep, and my blanket was suddenly wet. It gave me the motivation to say, "Here is where I am, nobody else can help my mother."

When I got to the sixth grade, most of my friends went to junior high, and in junior high they learned English, which was very impressive. When we were talking, they would say, "You are a dog, you are a cat." They used English words to impress people. I said, "Why am I behind them?" So I decided to take evening classes at the junior high. I went to my sixth-grade class from seven to noon, then I went home from noon to three, then from three to five I had to go to school in the afternoon. Immediately after five, five-thirty, they gave evening classes. So I was taking those classes—English, history, math. . . . I really worked hard, and I worked late. I didn't have a table. I didn't have a chair. But I did have an oil lamp. I lay on the bed reading, and sometimes I fell asleep. When I fell asleep, my mother took my book and put it in my bag.

I flunked my national exam when I was in sixth grade, even though I had very good grades. That's a long story. It is very well known in my country that there are wizards, or marabous, people who have extra powers who can help you get good grades, whether you are a good student or not. At that time I believed in them. So when my mother gave me a charm, I put it in my pocket and pressed it. I believed that everything I was going to write, even if it was wrong, would be correct. Then when I took the exam, I refused to think, and I flunked the test. I thought the marabou was behind me, in the air, and was going to help me; but I flunked.

I had to repeat the sixth grade for one more year; but I learned a lot. Even though I'd had very good grades, there were things I hadn't understood; and things went very well after that. I went to the seventh grade, and I already had knowledge in math, chemistry, English, geography, natural science. . . . Everything was fine; everything went quickly. My apartment was full of friends who came to ask me questions. I was really happy.

Then I realized how hard my mother was working to pay my tuition and buy me clothes. In the ninth grade, I decided to work during the summer for a carpenter. I woke up at 6:30 and made bricks and cement from 7:00 to 3:00 every day. I was getting paid fifteen cents a day.

For people in my country, making bricks is a dirty job. The first week I was working, I saw girls from my class coming and I hid myself. I didn't want the girls to see me. Later, I talked to my mother, and she said, "No, you are not stealing money. You are not doing something wrong. You are working, and you should be proud of yourself." You see? Then, the next day, I would like all my friends to see me, and they came and talked to me.

I worked for two or three months, and I saved enough money to buy a bicycle. Most of my friends had bicycles. Then I thought, "No, my mother is working hard for me"; so I gave all my money to my mother.

After I graduated from high school, and then college, I was supposed to go to the military service, and then after that I was supposed to teach. But I had the feeling that I had the potential to go somewhere to get a doctoral degree. I wanted a Ph.D. I wanted to do research and work to improve the school system in Burkina Faso. When I got accepted to the University of Iowa, I bought the ticket with money I'd saved from teaching while I was working on my baccalaureate degree, but I still needed a passport. At that time, the government didn't allow students to leave the country. I had to pretend to be a civil servant. A friend wrote me a letter saying I was going to work in his office and that I had to go to Marseilles, France, for training. I got a passport to go to Marseilles, but I could have gone to jail, and my friend could have, too. He risked his life.

When I left my country, it was December 24, 1986. I arrived in New York on December 29. I was outside. I had a nasty coat with a hat like a big clown from Paris. I was cold. I was hungry. I went to buy coffee. All the people were watching me as if I were someone who just fell from the sky.

When I arrived in Iowa City, I had twenty-five dollars left. Although a friend here loaned me some money, it was very difficult to find an apartment. There was one woman who didn't like to rent to blacks. When she saw me, she said, no, I was too tall to rent her apartment. I slept on a tiny couch in a rented room for the first semester. That was not so bad, but then came the cold weather of Iowa City. My coat sleeves were too short, and I had to cover my arms with my socks. It was very cold. The food was tough. My English was bad. Oh my goodness! Everything was difficult. Still, in 1989, I got my master's in applied math. Then I moved to chemistry, and I'm going to finish my Ph.D. sometime this year.

This is the story of one man's entire life: work. Every hour, he works against a debt owed to a young boy who slept with mud on his head, who forewent soccer and sleep and summers with friends — and to a mother who believed in the marabou, loved him, and "had nothing." It is a bond that comes due after the next task is finished, or the next one. He cannot very well let that boy and his mother down after all these years. What will those lost summers be worth, after all, if he does not finish this job? Weighed against those summers and those nights, the hours I wait become light, float off like balloons.

But in some ways our fears are similar: He is afraid of losing hours and pleasures already spent, already forfeited, to a future that is still on its way. I am afraid of losing the hours and pleasures I have left to someone who does not appreciate the significance of the gift.

It is a difficult balance. Still, I have been considering this possibility: Sometimes there really are extenuating circumstances.

I don't know.

Even as I write this, Hassimi is in the process of being late. We were supposed to go to a party together at three. We decided to go at four, and he has just called to tell me he will be a few minutes late. "Some women from Togo," he tells me, "want to go to the grocery store," and he could not take them earlier because he was working. He will drop me off at the party, rush back here to get the women, take them to the store, and then return to the party. He thinks he can do all this in an hour, is still so optimistic. He does not think about the lines at the grocery store, the things that will not be available at Econofoods, the student he will see in aisle three, the cashier that will recognize him and want to chat.

When we first began seeing each other, I drew pictures of him in my letters to friends — a tall man bending his head down to listen to someone at the grocery store, in the parking lot, on the street. Sometimes I just drew a sunflower with its neck arched downward and its petals radiating heat or a tree with long, delicate fingers. There was something silent there, something both accepting and unmoving that I was drawn to, that I continue to be drawn to. Sometimes I think he could listen forever to my complaints about his absence, his preoccupation, his lateness, without ever being swayed to follow my clock, to work more according to my ideas about boundaries, about work, about saying "no" — but also without ever leaving me, without judging or dismissing or ceasing his attempts to understand me.

I have noticed this: in the presence of Hassimi's silence my voice gets louder. I hear myself speaking more vociferously and with more assurance. I get angry more easily; I am bossier; I blunder more noisily and with more open embarrassment when I am speaking French — and when I am speaking English. If a certain fumbling bluntness, a certain self-assuredness, are American, then, ironically, I am more American with Hassimi. At least, I am more unapologetically American.

And then sometimes there is a change. It is true. Hassimi is more consistently on time. There are weeks when I have no complaint, when I see him every day, when he is emotionally available to me. I noticed just yesterday that the telephone was turned off all night. The night before we had watched a movie together. Today he called me to plan lunch for Wednesday. And I, whether he can see it or not, have been trusting him more, making kinder assumptions about the reasons he is gone. I try to plan time with him that is more utilitarian — going to the grocery store, making food for the week, writing letters home — things we both need to do but can do together. What if, I ask myself, this were not just white bourgeois America? What if it were some more difficult circumstance? What if it were some important struggle? For Hassimi, of course, it is.

AT THE
TEMPLE

Jessie Carroll Grearson

he first time I walked into the temple in
Aurora, I forgot to take off my shoes. I
pulled open the heavy doors and started
to step inside, which brought Viren
running in from the field where he'd
been smoking a cigarette. It was chilly
inside, and smelled of incense and straw
flowers, and some other unnameable Indian scent that I know
but cannot place, something as piercing as camphor, but sweeter,
sort of like licorice, anise. By then Viren had arrived, and I had
discarded my white Reeboks by the small pile of Indian leather
sandals. My socks, I noticed, had holes in the toes, and the car-
pet was thin over what felt like a cement floor.

There was an outer room with niches in it, and in these niches
were gods and goddesses. Kali I recognized, a small goddess in

black with a bright red tongue: goddess of protection and re-
venge. Then Lakshmi, to whom you pray for wealth and pros-
perity. Then a god whose name I don't remember, with an
elephant face and long almond-shaped Indian eyes, curving
around his head. Before each figure in the god-niches were what
I figured were offerings: coconut halves, butter in small golden
bowls, flowers, rice. At each alcove Viren stopped, closed his
eyes, and raised his hands together, bowing his head.

"Are you praying in Hindi?" I asked.

"In Kutchi," he replied.

We went into the big central room. The windows were square
and uncurtained, with freshly strung garlands of flowers in yellows, reds, and pinks. I think there may have been more gods,
but I don't remember for sure because by then I'd seen the *pièce
de résistance*, Balaji, the more-than-life-size golden and bejew-
eled statue placed in an alcove beyond a man garbed in only
some white cotton cloth wrapped around his waist and legs. The
man was holding a brass bowl, standing behind a box clearly
meant to take offerings. I saw Viren put in what looked like
a $20 bill. I must have looked surprised, because he said, "I
haven't been in a long time."

There was a woman on the floor before the statue. She got
up in a fluid motion and the man blessed her; she warmed
her hands at an oil lamp then moved them up over her face as
though washing herself in the glow of the flame. By then a
group of us had collected. The priest began pouring something from the bowl, something to drink, into each of our
hands. A semicircle of hands (one-potato, two-potato — I
thought briefly of the childhood game where we counted out
who was to be it), my white hands held out just like theirs.
He began to pour into my hands and then stopped, saying
something I didn't understand. Viren translated: I wasn't holding my hands properly, they didn't make a waterproof cup.
So I put one over the other and drank — water flavored with
something — something like that unnameable Indian smell,
otherworldly.

Then he marked our foreheads with a powder that was red and pollenlike. It stayed on for the whole afternoon.

2

This story begins at a table. Indian food, eaten in London or in Oxford. Dark, narrow restaurants, sitting low at a table, eating things awkwardly with my fingers, my mouth hot, the flavors unfamiliar, startling. The cold taste of *lassi*—a reward for making it to the end of the meal—tart, yoghurty, with a hint of something else. Lime? Vanilla? Later I learned: essence of rose.

Or perhaps it begins in fourth grade, with Mrs. McClymon making us some flat wholewheat bread fried in butter—I remember the bread, and more hazily, the world map, with her pointing to the wedge of India, surrounded by pale blue water. Or perhaps earlier still, at bedtime, when my mother read us chapters from *The Secret Garden*. Mary, the heroine, lived in India, had an Ayah.

Pieces, fragments, waiting to be important, to be used later, fit into the mosaic. History read backwards as pattern. If it wasn't for Viren, would I ever have recovered any of it?

I don't remember being especially interested in or attracted to India before I met Viren. And yet I did consider myself attracted to other cultures—but what did that mean? In college, I went to the international center for hours, reading over leaflets and brochures, longing for something other, but it was unnamed. I hadn't taken another language (only Latin, in high school), so I decided to love English all the more, made it my focus, ended up in England for six months. Another culture, yes—but so safe.

Farther back. What other cultures were there in the small New Hampshire town in which I lived for the first eighteen years of my life? There was only my friend Julio César Ortiz, from Guatemala (who introduced me to the word "xenophobic," in relation to our small town and private school). The word waited in my mind for years, unrecovered.

I met Viren at the end of summer. We were eating soup together at a restaurant called the Farmer's Market. I'd tagged
along with friends of mine who were getting a ride to a Wisconsin lake with him. We all had a bowl of their spicy soup. Our
eyes watered. His glinted with a silent amusement. "Don't you
think this is hot?" we asked him.

"No."

"And this is all mild," he said, later, pointing to the dishes
spread out over the rickety table in his Dodge Street, Iowa City,
apartment, "so help yourselves." There were spiced eggs, stuffed
peppers, rice with vegetables, ground beef with peas, lentil soup.
Yoghurt with cucumbers. "Help yourselves," he said. We did.

I took a little of everything, tasted several bites of the mild
stuff feeling sophisticated and curious, inspecting the flavor like
a connoisseur when — impact — the heat hit my tongue, invol-
untary tears rolled down my face. He was distressed.

"This was to be *mild*," he repeated, perplexed, apologetic.
And went to get me water.

I don't know how it was, then, that he could so like the food
at the Amana Colonies. Its main feature is abundance; there
is nothing so bland in my recent culinary experience. But we
found ourselves there, on what turned out to be our first date.
Mid-October 1988. Brunch. Eggs, pancakes, potatoes, bread,
butter, fruit. The most exotic flavorings: cinnamon and black
pepper. He told me he was finishing school, leaving in December. I said, "Don't." The word seemed startled out of me, surprising us both.

As surprised as we both were when, as I teetered walking
along on the railroad tracks after the meal, he put his arm
around me to steady me. And left it there.

3

First he taught me how to make Indian tea: a cup of milk
(whole), a cup of water. Three teaspoons of the loose tea, two

teaspoons of sugar. A little dust of cardamom. Boil it until it rises, three times, pour it through a sieve.

Then he taught me to cook a few dishes, frying the spices first in oil, separately. Slow down, don't rush things. I would come over and watch him slice onions, tiny, methodically cut slices. I could do it in half the time, with onion pieces twice as big.

I learned that *sabji* meant vegetables for dinner and that I was always invited. I learned how to make spiced rice with cloves, green peas, and cardamom pods. I learned that *papad* (a thin, salty lentil wafer, roasted) was available at East-West grocery stores. That *dal* was the necessary lentil soup. *Keema*, ground beef with peas. And *bhindi* (okra) was good with potatoes.

"More," I said, "teach me more!"

"That's all I know," he said.

Later, we picked out an Indian cookbook for me by Madhur Jaffrey at Prairie Lights bookstore. I felt excited, but nervous.

I tried to figure it out later, as we stood over the stove in my kitchen, waiting for the tea to boil together, standing there quietly without the lights on, mesmerized by the blue of the gas flame, and the blue of the moonlight on the kitchen floor. Why? I tried to step outside the moment, look at it objectively, see it as it might be seen later: was the cookbook another sign, a piece of the pattern? Or something I was playing at, fooling myself with, something I'd look at later with skepticism or sorrow, a discarded reminder.

We saw each other every day, mostly in the evenings, after I had finished with my long day taking classes and teaching. I taught six days out of seven that semester, Monday through Saturday, and had classes four days a week. I was always busy, except around dinnertime. I spent hours in the evenings at Viren's apartment.

I went there to get away from all that busy academic confusion (though always my book bag came with me, heavy with books and student papers that, I refused to notice, again and again, I never even unpacked).

Escape—perhaps that was the word for it, the initial attraction of his apartment, which he shared with his friend Ravi. I remember it as full of people, mostly men, friends who would just walk in, drift in one or two at a time, somehow collect — and when some critical point was reached, someone would make tea. Or dinner, depending on what time it was. Familiar, at ease, they'd joke about whose turn it was, tease each other, laughing.

I was delighted, intrigued. Hadn't seen that kind of easygoing closeness, people connecting without making a plan first. And that apartment was meant to accommodate such occasions — three or four dilapidated ("well-used") chairs, a couch, pillows. It could take it. (Viren never mentioned my own lack of such furnishings: my apartment, high-ceilinged, sparsely furnished, no couch, a rocking chair. He walked around in it quietly, looking at paintings and photographs, picking up objects of ornament with his careful hands.) I'd try to imagine inviting them all over to my place, but couldn't. For one thing, where would they all sit? My living room was suited mostly for intimate conversations, one to one.

They certainly could accommodate me better than I could them — which is what they did.

I blew into Viren's life so suddenly, entirely unannounced, and yet no one really commented; they just increased their dinner plans by a half cup of rice, by another teaspoon of tea, another chair pulled up, or another cushion on the floor. Not just Viren's roommate, Ravi (who was always kind to me), but the whole system (which I was beginning to see was extensive) flexed and adjusted with hardly a ripple. *Bring Jessie along.*

I spent hours at their apartment, practicing. Just being — with them, with him. Just being myself.

"Do you like to be busy all the time?"

Viren would ask me this, not with judgment, but with real curiosity. Perhaps a touch of amusement. And I would ask myself that question sometimes, as I tried to rest and be like them, relaxed, doing nothing, eating together, looking forward to eating together, chatting about nothing in particular. Just being together. Being.

Sometimes—when I was tired enough—I could almost manage it. As though a big, central spring in me unwound one careful notch. As though I could accept the seconds more slowly, each one an inhalation, a pleasure, not a responsibility.

Their voices fascinated me (they stopped speaking Hindi when I was around), but I would try to get Viren to speak to me in one of his several other languages. "You don't understand," he'd say. "It's hard to talk to you when you don't understand." Still, I'd listen when he and Ravi forgot about me and slipped into their common language, Hindi; sometimes I'd let the language flow over me like a stream (the intonations and inflections that sounded not-quite-English now part of the pattern of sound, at home), sometimes I'd try to hold onto individual words and phrases, writing them down, practicing.

Once we were playing Scrabble, and I saw the perfect opportunity to impress them and to use my two U's. U-l-d-u, I proudly spelled, and sat back waiting for their appreciation. They looked puzzled.

"You know," I prompted, "Uldu, like that poem I always try and get you to say."

Oh, *Urdu*—they laughed and corrected me. Ravi suggested how I could still use my two U's—with the word *ullu.*

"It means 'fool' in Hindi."

4

Phoolon ki ruth hai, thandi havaen.

That's what the first line of the poem (written in Urdu) sounds like to me, though I can't remember the rest except in translation.

It means, "The air smells of flowers, cool breezes." Then:

> Her choice, now, whether or not she comes.
> If you stay among flowers,
> if you live among flowers—

how can you save your hem
from thorns?

It was late autumn. We'd had a misunderstanding. When we straightened it out, when we were comfortable again, he translated the poem for me, wrote it down so I could keep it. On the back of a business card at the Country Kitchen, his elaborate shapes and curlicues, my English translation. I loved the poem; it captured something for me, something I was beginning to see, something tugging at me.

I was beginning to see what was tugging at him. His family. His need to leave Iowa City and get on with his life. ("Won't you miss it here?" / "Not really—I don't get attached to places.") To "begin his life," an activity that I later realized included finding a wife, starting a family.

That poem changed our relationship. Indirectly it named something—something of our dilemma, its possible outcome. The dawning of real differences—not just the colorful, fascinating ones, but the real differences that hurt, caused difficulties. It was as though those cool winds of the poem blew over each of us, as though in that moment of chill we had each seen our choices laid out matter-of-factly: together or apart.

At that time it was not clear what would become of us.

The first time we went to Devon Avenue in Chicago was the first time Viren refused to hold my hand. He just shook his head no, apologetic but firm. There it was—little India. I was fascinated as I wove in and out of the grocery stores, with their cardboard boxes of vegetables: the long, pale-green, squashlike vegetable; the small, oval, striped vegetables that looked like tiny watermelons; the bunches of cilantro and heaps of ginger root and garlic and coconuts. The dusty boxes of spices, soaps, and teas that looked aged, as though the store had been caught in a time warp. The spellings on the shop signs: *sarees, saris,* and my favorite description on one restaurant, "Pakistani Cousin."

But something was making me sad. We dodged into some European cafe, stranded and pathetic in the middle of colorful and bustling Devon Avenue. We sat in a window booth, and I watched Indian women go by: gaily dressed older women with long gray braids and bright red silks; young women in *churidar kurtas*, high heels, and shining gold jewelry; middle-aged women carrying dark-eyed babies with long, long eyelashes and black hair. Family groupings, no one alone.

For six months, we had seen each other almost every day. In some old-fashioned, restrained way, we had courted, never once saying, I love you.

"I don't want you to marry an Indian woman," I said. The words felt forced out, painful.

"You do realize," he asked me, "what you're saying."

5

If you make up your minds, stick to it.

That is what I heard his parents say to me over the phone the first time we spoke, the odd bouncing echo, the occasional word disappearing, sinking into the ocean (oceans) between us. That sentence stood whole and clear, spoken by his father.

"*Haji,*" Viren said. "Yes, sir," I whispered.

At the beginning of our relationship, we always seemed to find ourselves at the end of the evening drinking coffee in Denny's or Maid-Rite. It was then that I tried to pull from Viren details of his life in India. He liked to talk about uncomplicated things — how good the cold water kept in clay pots tasted after the heat; how good his mother's cooking had tasted to him after boarding-school fare; how he had spent whole Saturdays in Bombay book markets lost in his reading, returning only for the evening meal. How he had lived on the edge of a jungle as a child, but that it had been eroded to almost nothing now. How the monkeys in India are bold and scary, how they haunt the temples and frighten children.

But I wanted him to talk about complicated things — like arranged marriages. He didn't like to discuss that with me, someone destined to misunderstand, destined for a "love marriage." For me, the subject had the fascination of a loose tooth. The strangeness of his explaining, even defending the logic of the system to *me*, his girlfriend, had a surreal quality that I liked. I wanted to make sense of it. *How* did it work?

Bit by bit I pieced it together: his family would pick girls for him to meet. Photographs would be exchanged, each family would carefully research the other, check horoscopes, and the two prospective partners, if there were no objections from the families, might meet for a date. If the two liked one another, they would marry. But no one, in Viren's family at least, was going to insist. Easy-going Viren — I tried to get my mind around this, tried to see him nodding agreeably, browsing among possible lives, selecting a photograph like a card from a deck — all right, I will marry her.

Over time, the concept of arranged marriages must have grown less foreign to me, because one day I actually found myself defending it to friends who wanted to know but were also slightly horrified. It's not *so* different, I offered. Think of how old-fashioned parents intervened and what they were checking for: compatible backgrounds, similar levels of education and finances. Was the family a good family? Was the person going to be treated well?

And the relief of not having all that responsibility to yourself! I have to admit that appealed to me too. To the part of me that so feared and had avoided making large decisions that involved other people's lives. Much better to spread the responsibility of the decision out, have it rest on other heads — older and wiser — than mine.

I had begun to feel the weight of our decision settling on me. For a little while, in the beginning, I had teased Viren for not telling his parents about me. I didn't want to be an experience he took back with him to India, a souvenir. I'd felt hurt, angry even, to be his secret American girlfriend. After all, he had met my parents the first Christmas after we met, and I had told them about him the weekend after our first date. What was the big deal?

But gradually I began to understand and began to appreciate the anonymity that allowed me to know them, even to listen to their voices without their knowing I existed. It gave me a secret power.

Viren never said so, but I knew he was worried about how they would take it. One of our friends was the eldest son of a conservative Indian family; they had refused to speak to him after he told them he was going to marry blonde, American Diane. Why tell them, why worry them until we were sure? And I still wasn't sure, was I?

I remember being attracted to Viren's way of making decisions, noticing that it was much more restful than my own sometimes fretful and haphazard way, that he was at peace with his decisions in a way that I never seemed to be with mine. Viren is an infinitely careful, thoughtful person, who approaches all decisions with the same deliberate consideration. His decisions are the result of an internal process and seem touched both by fate and commitment to a final plan.

The first time I witnessed this process, I had agreed to help him purchase a suitcase — something I hadn't realized would take not an afternoon but a week. First, visit all the stores that carried the idea of a suitcase he was looking for. Compare the prices and values at the five stores. Repeat the visit to the five stores. Decide, wait a few days, then purchase the best value for the money. ("What are you waiting for? Just get it — you can always return it." / "You're so *im*patient," he told me, when one round of the stores was good enough for me and I was ready to go home. "Why are you so *im*patient?")

For me, decision making, when not hasty, was more hypothetical; as I made my way toward an important decision, I would try on possibilities, often subjecting them to endless rounds of scrutiny and discussions with friends, knowing what I wanted by hearing what I said, noticing how often my mind and words changed depending on the person I was talking to. I would try so hard to have thought of everything, to be absolutely sure, that my decisions were often the result of exhaustion.

And this decision had global significance. It put me like a small stone, with ripples spreading outward, at the center—and I was afraid. Afraid to decide about us, afraid to say to him, change your life for me, leave your country. Find a job here, marry me.

I hadn't always been careful, and I didn't have a serene belief in fate, and I was afraid of marriage, afraid of making a choice, of disrupting so many lives. My own life. (Indian marriages weren't like American ones—there was no understood "return policy" of divorce, I could tell.) I was afraid of disrupting Viren's relationship with his family, which seemed to me to be astonishingly close, sweet, and untroubled. And so we waited.

In the end, it was Viren's sister, Deepa, who arranged our marriage. Viren had driven down to Alabama to visit her in her home there, and within minutes she had pulled his secret from him. He must have already decided, had been ready to tell her, to begin. The next day, I was on a southbound flight for a long-weekend visit, summoned to meet her and her husband, Satish.

I was nervous. Things, I suspected, had been set in motion, and I no longer had the power to stop them. When I met Deepa, when she draped her arms around my shoulders and said nice things about me in English and in Kutchi, I knew that I was right. It was my first taste of instant Indian love, and I was feeling it too—falling down into some infinitely soft place, engulfed, sleepy, accepted, forever. Deepa in the doorway of her home inviting me in, the light spilling out, her soft brown arm draped over my shoulders, her beautiful face, and the door closing behind us.

Viren made Deepa promise not to tell their parents, but she eventually broke that promise, intervened. Deepa, who herself had an arranged marriage but the heart of a romantic, knew fate when she saw it. She had said to Viren in Kutchi, *your face is blossoming*. She couldn't stand the suspense of her parents' continuing their preliminary search for a wife with whom Viren would begin his life, sending over phone numbers of girls for Viren to call, their calling and asking her in Kutchi: what was going on? So she, being sure enough for all of us, and knowing her brother's heart, took matters into her own hands.

I don't know what that first call was like, what Viren's parents really said to Deepa or to one another. I can imagine though, the translation, "Are you sure?" How they must have thought but perhaps not said, "Who will take care of us in our old age, the eldest son's job?" Both of their children gone to America. But they wanted their son to be happy, they wanted his happiness most of all — so they told me later, when they visited. Two years after our marriage I could see they were still getting over the astonishment, still laughing at the memory of their own surprise — Viren was such a quiet boy! Very uneventful! Very obedient. They hadn't expected this from *him*.

Viren had written to them; his letter seemed to me so full of respect for them, concern for their feelings, so old-fashioned. In it he described each member of my family, documenting their jobs, their educational achievements. Establishing that we were a good family.

I got my first letter from them on my birthday. It was a pretty hand-printed card and bore the message, *Jaysi ho, achchhi ho,* which I knew played off my name. The Indian friend to whom I read it tried to translate its meaning: *As you are, you are ours.* Or, As you are, we accept you. Or, Whatever you are, you're good. "It's really hard to translate — it is more accepting than I'm making it sound — "

I felt thrilled and terrified, and tried to describe to him the feeling: that some door had swung wide; that I had stepped into a room full of people and was distracted, delighted, and dimly aware that the door was swinging shut; that my last chance to leave was leaving me. "I feel like they are welcoming me in," I said. "Forever."

"Well, that's exactly right, that's the thing about Indian families," Satyajit Chatterjee explained to me, laughing. "You can absolutely count on them to always be there for you. But that's the thing. They'll *always* be there."

6

"I think we are serious," I remember saying from the backseat of a car. My parents were taking me to the airport; I was flying back to Iowa, to Viren. I waited for a reply. I knew we were serious, but I suddenly realized that I had been so focused on Viren's parents' reactions that I had forgotten to fill my own parents in. I had updated my parents occasionally but had not given them much indication that this relationship was different from any of the others.

My parents didn't seem terribly surprised or ruffled, but they hesitated, and I noticed that. They liked Viren, my mother began. He is a very nice *person.*

My mother is a very widely read and well-educated woman. My father takes his cues from my mother. I got the sense that they had rehearsed this part. But they didn't go on.

I doubt we'll live in India, I offered, seeking to reassure them.

But what are his *interests*, my mother asked me.

I sat back, stunned, unable to answer.

What interests, what hobbies did we share? We both liked to read. We liked to cook together. We didn't *do* that much together really, besides cook and talk and walk around holding hands and looking at the world together. An arrow, the kind only parents can send, pierced my heart, shook my provisional certainty.

I realize now that they were simply expressing concern over our different backgrounds — a difference no one defined, but that everyone referred to as "the cultural thing" — that perhaps this was even an obligatory remark and one they will not even remember. But because I had been looking so hard toward India, because I had taken my parents' support for granted and had not thought about their own reactions and concerns, I was unsettled.

Later, troubled, I discussed this conversation with my Korean friend, also married to an Indian. "Hobby," Hygene mused. "Seems very American idea. What is he interested in? I would say he is interested in *you*."

At my Iowa City wedding, I felt my family close around me, like a full tide. What were they thinking? I didn't know. But they were there for me, doing for me, finishing what I hadn't been able to finish. The programs, the decorations. Helping out.

That first wedding, in a little Iowa City church, I could hardly get out my vows. My heart seemed to balk in front of the ceremony's big symbols, and everything pressed in on me. We taped the ceremony and Viren's voice booms out his vows with a loving certainty to my painful whisper. I felt as though all the joy and pain of my life constricted my throat to a prism through which that whisper was refracted.

To me, in a chauvinistic, American way, this was the *real* wedding, the one I had planned, the one that counted. That all *my* people would be at. The one *my* family would attend. To be fair, that we would have an Indian ceremony in the United States was decided much later, at the very last minute, after plane tickets to the Midwest had been purchased, vacation days arranged. But when I think back on how my parents-in-law arranged the whole event in another country from their son's apartment, when I think that only my mother attended, in ret- rospect, though I understand how I let this happen, I feel ashamed.

7

Seeing the temple in Aurora, Illinois, from Interstate 88 always seems lucky to me. One of the few interesting sights on the commute between Iowa City and Chicago, it is located in the middle of a field, maybe an eighth of a mile off the highway. It comes up very quickly after an underpass; Viren always nudges me to attention—you won't see it unless you are looking. To me, the spires on it look like the elaborate tops of sand castles, dribbled by hand.

Looking at it, moving my body to keep it in sight for as long as I can while going sixty miles an hour, I can smell the inside of it, the way memory sometimes travels from the outside in as scent, up through the nose into the head, the smell of India blooms in my mind and becomes the cool of the basement around me where the ceremony took place.

I am wrapped in a heavy aqua silk sari, with gold embroidery. Deepa has expertly, carefully, pleated the yards of fabric into classic sari folds, and I have watched, helplessly, knowing I cannot remember how to do it, working like that from the outside in, tucking and draping. I am feeling uncertain and somehow diffuse, grateful for the tight fitting silk blouse that seems to hold me together and in place. I am a balloon that would float away if it were not for the ten inches of gold and glass bangles on each arm, the weight of the sari's gold edge, the jewels and flowers in my hair, around my throat. Even the makeup on my face and the pattern of red and gold that Deepa's careful, pretty hands have gently pressed onto my forehead feel like they hold a mask in place, the heaviness of a mask donned for a solemn occasion.

My own mother is there, dressed in a gold costume, a wedding present for me that is too large. We sit together; Viren is having some private ceremony with the priest, sitting cross-legged and shirtless, his head bent with the priest as though in private conversation. There is music—"No wonder," I thought fleetingly, "Viren likes Bob Dylan." The taped sitar music was quite Dylan-like, atonal and whiny. Mysterious. Unexpectedly moving.

And I am nervous, more nervous suddenly than for the first ceremony, the one I had arranged, that we had practiced. I don't want to disappoint anyone, but I don't know what I'm doing.

The wedding will be conducted in Sanskrit, so Viren doesn't know either. And his parents, the most diplomatic but determined people in the world suddenly—who have been forced to have a priest from the South, not from their own community—well, I want to be a good sport like them. I see how much this means to them, I feel such a responsibility as I wait for the auspicious moment, that which has been determined by the stars and by both of our birth times.

I step up onto the little wedding stage decked gaily with streamers and side-by-side portraits of Viren's grandparents with garlands of flowers. What am I doing? What will happen? I face a pink cotton cloth; I know that on the other side Viren is facing me, and briefly I think of a long-ago Hindu bride who, only as the cloth was dropped at the right moment, would finally get to see the face of her groom, her life-mate.

But the curtain drops, and it is Viren's familiar face that I see, and everything is better as we exchange garlands. This ceremony is not sad—there is laughter and talking; Viren is seated next to me. I see the American guests in the audience, after a few uncertain smiles, begin to relax, too, to realize that one can get up and move around at an Indian wedding, that these things take a while, that they can discuss among themselves what it is we are doing up there on that stage with those two coconuts surrounded by rice and flowers, waving our hands over brass pots of oil, rice, and betel nuts, pouring wheat into the fire.

My self-consciousness fades and I feel warm, happy. As though the first wedding was a rehearsal for this, for me the symbols are transformed into meaning, translation unnecessary. We cup our hands into a waterfall and the priest pours water down over them, from one family into another; we are joined together. Incense wafts into our hair and eyes, stinging, but the heavy *mangalsutra* wedding necklace is placed around my neck; it is the right weight, serious, but reassuring and comforting too. We walk around the fire seven times; we journey connected by our joined hands and by the pink cloth tied to the hem of my sari, draped over Viren's shoulder. We bow before our relatives;

they touch our shoulders. Respect. We feed each other sweets out of a Tupperware container; we will always feed each other. Our vows are in Sanskrit—a language neither of us knows—so it is the sound of each other's voices we hear and smile at, nod to.

At the end of the evening, my mother-in-law placed in our hands the two yellow chrysanthemum garlands we had worn. She instructed us to throw them into a "big river." So we carried them back to the Iowa River and waited until it was night and the river was black and high and the lights slipped over its surface. We each took one, and we threw them out toward the middle where the current moved like a slow, deep muscle. Lifting the weight and letting go, I imagined the arc they made traveling through the air before the dim, anticipated splash-thunk as they landed in the river, beginning their journey.

Settling

YEARNING
TO
BREATHE
FREE

Le Ly Hayslip

onolulu's warm breeze caressed me like a mother's hands. A pretty hula girl put a flowered lei — a victor's garland — around my neck. For the first time in my life, I gulped the heady air of a world at peace.

May 27, 1970, the day I stepped onto the ramp at Honolulu International Airport after fleeing the war in Vietnam, marked the beginning of my new life as an apprentice American. It may have been my imagination, but the attendants on the big American jetliner from Saigon seemed exceptionally kind to me and my two boys — three-year-old Jimmy (whose father, a wealthy Saigon industrialist, he never knew) and Tommy, the three-month-old son of my new American husband, Ed Munro, whom we were on our way to join. Liberty and goodwill, like corruption and cruelty, seem to hold each other's hand.

Still, Hawaii was too much like Vietnam to really count as the United States. For one, it was a tropical island—covered with palms and sand—and Honolulu, despite its modern hotels and shops and restaurants, was too much like Saigon: filled with Asians and GIs, tawdry bars and taxis, and people in transit, *khong hieu qua khu*—without a past or future, like me. The thrill of great America would have to wait for our next landing.

As it turned out, San Diego was another Honolulu, written on a larger page. Our plane arrived after midnight, not a good time for sightseeing, especially by timid immigrants. In Vietnam, the Viet Cong feared the light, so "friendly" areas—cities, towns, air bases, and outposts—were lit up like American Christmas trees. Perhaps to show it was safe for GIs coming back from the war, San Diego, too, left its lights burning all night.

Ed met us at the arrival gate, just as he'd promised. He had been staying with his mother, Erma, in the suburb of El Cajon. Although he looked tanned and healthy and was a welcome familiar face after thousands of miles of strangers, my heart sagged when I saw him. Born in 1915 (seven years after my mother's birth) in Mount Vernon, Washington, he was old enough to be my father—no twenty-year-old's dream husband. Yet, with two brothers and three sisters, he was no stranger to small towns and big families—one reason, in addition to his own maturity, that he understood me so well. His mother had been a waitress at something called a "drive-in" and his father, like mine, had died. Both had been honest, family-loving men who tackled life barehanded. My father had been a farmer who seldom went farther than a day's walk from our home village of Ky La. Ed's dad had been a carpenter and hunter who ventured to Alaska: a wondrous place where, Ed said, ice fell stinging from the sky. In all, Ed's relatives were solid working-class people. Like my peasant family, they loved one another, loved their country, and lived their values every day.

Ed had been married twice before. He knew, as I did, how it felt to lose the game of love. His first wife gave him two sons, Ron and Ed, Jr. (navy boys whom we visited in Vietnam), then divorced him and moved to Nevada. His second wife was unfaithful, and when Ed found out about it, he did not beat her as a Vietnamese husband would but sent her a dozen roses and wished her good luck with her new man. In a way, that was what Ed was all about. He put the wishes of those he loved above his own right to be happy. This constant sacrifice, I think, whittled him down and eventually cost him what he treasured most. In this, I would discover, he was not alone among Americans.

The long drive from San Diego's Lindbergh Field to El Cajon was not much different from a drive to Saigon's suburbs, except for more cars and fewer motorbikes on the highway's six broad lanes. Off the freeway, we drove through blocks of tidy homes, all dark except for streetlamps standing like GI basketball hoops in the gloom. We parked in the driveway of a pale yellow house — "ranch style," Ed said, although I couldn't smell any animals — and we went up the narrow walk to a front door bright with light. Before Ed could reach the bell, a shadow hobbled up behind the curtain. The door opened onto a large American woman in curlers, backlit in a nightgown as big as a sheet.

Startled, I bowed low — to be polite and to put the big creature out of sight while I collected my sleep-starved wits.

"Ohhh!" Erma, Ed's sister, screamed, slapping her cheeks, and pulling me to her with beefy arms. "She's so cute — like a little china doll! I want to hug her to pieces!"

She very nearly did — a big, sloppy American bear hug, a show of emotion no proper Vietnamese would dare display on first meeting. It amazed me how quick Americans were to show affection to strangers, even those their menfolk had gone so far from home to destroy.

"And the children — ?" Erma peeked around my helmet of ratted hair. Ed had shown her pictures of my two sons.

"In the car!" He poked a dad's boastful thumb over his shoulder.

"Ooo—I can't wait to see them!" Erma scuttled down the walk. "I'll just eat them up!"

Eat them up—my god! Of course, it was just another American figure of speech. I was beginning to discover that English was as full of booby traps as the jungle outside Ky La.

Anyway, Ed's new family impressed her, for better *and* for worse. Jimmy was cranky from crossing time zones, and since he spoke mostly Vietnamese, he cried when this giant brown-haired bear-lady tried to crush him with her paws. Tommy, however, who had slept fourteen hours on the plane and was ready for fun, screeched with delight. Erma knew right away which boy had the bright, upstanding, red-white-and-blue American father and which child was the pitiful third-world refugee. First impressions are lasting. I think that midnight meeting forever biased her in Tommy's favor, although I never dreamed of saying it.

We unloaded the luggage and put the boys to bed, where I stayed with them until they fell asleep. From the depths of this strange-smelling, thick-walled American house, I listened to Ed and Erma chat in too fast English over coffee. I still didn't know what to make of my new environment: American kitchens smelled like sickly hospitals, reeking of disinfectant, not *Ong Tao* ("Mr. Stove's") healthy food. The darkness outside the house was as terrifying as a midnight cadre meeting. I wanted to join them and gossip and laugh like real family, but I understood only a fraction of what they said and part of that was whispered, which to me meant danger, not good manners. Fortunately, the deep, even breathing of the kids won me over and I fell asleep, reminding myself to pay special attention to any spirits who might visit me in my first American dream.

My first full day as an American housewife didn't go so well. I slept poorly in Erma's tight-sealed house, and my body still awoke and made water and got hungry on Saigon time. Nobody explained jet lag to me and I thought my strange waves of sleepiness in the middle of the day and spunkiness at four in the morning were just signs of how out of place Orientals were in round-eyed America. I hoped it would pass, like the flu, without my having to consult the neighborhood psychic or witch doctor.

My alarm clock on that first day was a playful slap on the rump.

"Get up, sleepyhead!" Ed yelled with a grin as wide as the band of sunlight streaming in through the window. He looked so happy to have his wife and family with him again that I thought he was going to burst. Like a slug in my mother's garden, I slithered around the sunburst to the shower, where I took another ten minutes to wake up.

I dressed and made up with great care, partly because of my new surroundings (unlike Vietnamese peasant houses, American homes have their owner's fingerprints all over them: no two housewives ever put wastebaskets and tissues in the same place!) and partly because I could take no chances with my appearance. Daylight and in-laws are terrible critics.

"Hurry up and dress the kids," Ed commanded. "After breakfast, I want you to meet my mother!"

In Vietnam, meeting in-laws is always a tricky business. This is true especially when the marriage has not been arranged through matchmakers and the couple are of vastly different ages, let alone races — *quen nhn ma, la nha chong,* I am at home in my mother's house, but a stranger to my in-laws! I would sooner have met an American battle tank on Erma's lawn than to walk next door unescorted and introduce myself to Ed's mother — which, for some unknown reason, was my husband's harebrained plan.

When Jimmy was dressed and fed (Tommy was still asleep and nobody had the courage to wake him), Ed booted us out and pointed to the shingled green house next door.

"Oh, go on!" he laughed. "You girls get acquainted. Mom won't bite your head off!"

Well, I certainly hoped not, but Ed hadn't met a real Vietnamese mother-in-law. Back in Danang, my mother had never accepted our marriage and so never treated Ed like a new family-member-in-training, with all the horror the position inspires. I dragged my son across the sunny lawn like a goat on the way to the slaughterhouse.

I squeezed Jimmy's spit-slick fingers and knocked on the door. Dogbarks from hell—we jumped back! The shadow of a big, Erma-like figure waddled toward us behind lacy curtains. A grandmother's high-pitched voice scolded the yappy dogs.

Had this been a Vietnamese house, I would have known instantly what to do. I would have bowed low, recited the ritual greeting of an unworthy daughter-in-law to the witch-queen who would transform me over the next few years into a deserving wife for her son, then gone into the kitchen and made us both some tea, humbly serving it with two hands, the old-fashioned way. Then I would have sat silently and waited to be instructed.

But this was an American house: a great sand-castle trap for a Vietnamese fish out of water. In Vietnam, a matchmaker would have prepared the way—sold my mother-in-law on my maidenly virtues, few as those might be. Now I would have to do my own selling, encumbered with my fatherless child, remembering how I had lost my virginity not once, but *three* times: bodily to the Viet Cong who raped me after my kangaroo court-martial; spiritually to Anh, Jimmy's father, with whom I fell into girlish love; and morally to the sad little GI in Danang who kept my family off the street by paying me four hundred U.S. dollars *green money* for a last happy memory of my country. By any measure, I was unworthy to stand on this fire-woman's stoop, let alone pretend to the honors and duties of a daughter-in-law. It was only because of my continuing bad karma that the earth did not swallow me up.

Despite my fears, the door opened onto the most angelic old face I had ever seen.

Leatha (whom I would always call "Mom Munro" and *never* impolitely by her first name) was seventy-five and had silver-blond hair that circled her cherub face the way white smoke twists around a storybook cottage. In Vietnam, such women aged like plucked berries: from the blush of virgin freshness to old age it was quick and downhill. Although a woman's post-birth *buon de* ritual, like our daily regimen of outdoor labor, kept our bodies lean and hard, we had no time or money for beauty treatments. Indeed, in a culture where reaching old age was a real accomplishment, we revered our elderly for being one step closer to the ancestors we worshiped. Old women and old men were sometimes mistaken for one another, and that was no cause for shame. In a way, this blending of sexes with its release from the trials of youth — concern for appearance and catching a mate — was one of aging's big rewards.

But not for Leatha.

Although Ed and Erma later assured me that she was "just an average grandma," I thought her angelic hair, well-fed happy face, plump saggy arms, solid girth, and movie star makeup made her even more spectacular than the painted Buddhas in the shrine beneath Marble Mountain near my village. Her appearance was even more astonishing, since in Vietnam I had seen no American women over fifty. (Most outsiders were men — soldiers or civilian contractors like Ed — or young female nurses.) Although her big hug made me feel better, I continued to stare at her. I tried to imagine my mother's face beneath the silver wreath and felt strangely envious and sad. Until I later found out how most Americans treat their elderly parents, the thought of growing old, fat, and pretty in America seemed to be another dividend of peace.

Of course, Leatha knew who I was at once and invited us inside. We talked only a minute before our polite smiles hurt and our rootless conversation slowed to head nods and empty laughter. I volunteered to make tea, but she insisted that was the hostess's duty. Unfortunately, such was my mood that even this unexpected kindness seemed like a slap in the face — a reminder of my foreignness and incapacity. How bad must a daughter-in-law be, I thought, not even to merit a stern lecture on family rules?

Eventually, Ed and Erma came over with Tommy and I felt more at ease. To be strictly proper, I should have sung the "new bride" song in the presence of both my husband and his mother — a kind of ceremonial acceptance of the collar of obedience:

> A risen moon is supposed to shine
> Except through clouds, when it is dim and weak,
> I come young and innocent to be your wife
> Please speak of me kindly in your mother's ear.
> People plant trees to grow big and strong,
> People have children to prosper and protect them.
> I cross my arms and bow my head
> To please my husband and his mother.
> If I do something wrong, please teach me right.
> Don't beat me or scold me in public
> For some will laugh and others will say
> The fist is my husband,
> The tongue is she from whence he came.

Instead, Ed put his arm around his mother and told her all about Vietnam, leaving out everything of importance in my black and bloody past — most of which he didn't know himself. Instead, he bragged about his mother's blue-ribbon pies at the Skagit Valley Fair, and I nodded enthusiastically, even though I hadn't the slightest idea what pies, blue ribbons, or county fairs really were. After Ed's father died, I learned, Leatha had moved south to California, where she took up residence next door with Erma, who shared a house with her husband, Larry, and adult son, Larry, Jr., who was seldom around.

I saw much more of her pixie-faced daughter, Kathy, a young woman about my age, who lived with her husband in the neighboring town of Santee. Why Leatha didn't move in with her daughter, who had more than enough room and could share housekeeping and cooking chores Vietnamese style, was beyond my understanding. I guessed that Americans loved their possessions so much that even a lonely old woman valued her own TV set, kitchen, bathroom, spare bedrooms, and garage for a car she couldn't drive more than living with a daughter in her sunset years.

Anyway, the longing in Leatha's eyes told me that she probably would have traded all her possessions for a little room among her family. Her "children" these days were six little dogs that jumped around like kids and yapped at the TV and pestered you for snacks and attention whenever you sat down. She even bought canned food for them at the store, which I thought was the height of decadence.

In Vietnam, a dog was a guardian first, then a pet, and sometimes dinner. It fed itself by foraging, not at the family's expense. I chalked up Leatha's behavior to American ignorance, and it helped me feel less like a bumpkin in their magnificent homes. After all, if they knew that the soul of a dog was really a transient spirit (usually a greedy person who had to earn a new human body by suffering a dog's life — most of it spent guarding someone else's wealth), they wouldn't be so quick to put them up on pedestals and deny them penance. I shuddered to think how Leatha's six "children" must have laughed among themselves in dogbark about their naive American mistress.

Ed and Leatha gossiped away the morning until Erma's son, Larry, joined us. I soon felt like the decorative china doll Erma had dubbed me when I arrived — just unwrapped and put on a shelf, worthy of an occasional glance but no conversation. Jet lag (as Ed now explained it) soon caught up with me again, and, depressed and exhausted, I bowed and apologized in Vietnamese, which I knew would sound more sincere, and went for a nap, leaving Ed to contend with the kids. I fell asleep wondering how quickly Ed's womenfolk would begin to complain about the "lazy new wife" he had brought to California.

When I awoke, most of our things had been moved from Erma's house to Leatha's. Ed preferred the company of his aged mom to imposing on his sister, and I agreed enthusiastically. Whereas Leatha seemed to look down on me as one of her puppies, Erma just seemed to look down. I was not prepared for this reversal of roles, for the sister-in-law was supposed to be the young bride's ally — someone who would comfort her when the rigors of wife training got too bad. In America, it seems, who you are is more important than the role society gives you. Even as Ed's wife, though, I did not seem to be worth too much.

That evening, Erma and Larry came over, and I tried to help the women fix dinner. Unfortunately, between my ignorance of American kitchens and a strong desire to avoid looking dumber than I had already, I didn't contribute much.

The first thing that astounded me was the refrigerator— a two-door monster that dwarfed our knee-high Vietnamese models—every nook and cranny of which was packed with food! It occurred to me that this was why Americans got so big: the bigger the refrigerators, the bigger the people. I thanked fate or luck or god that Jimmy would now grow up to be twice the size of Anh, his wealthy Vietnamese father. For a second I held a fantasy reunion: me, more rich and beautiful than Lien (Ahn's wife who had thrown me out of their mansion when I got pregnant); my mother—plump and queenly as Leatha; and Jimmy—called Phung Quoc Hung in Vietnamese—tall and powerful as an American Green Beret, stooping to shake his father's little hand. It was a scene that could never come true, although, as everybody said, all things are possible in America.

Erma took out a frosty box with the picture of a glowering green giant (no doubt a character from American fables who devoured children who didn't eat their vegetables), then a slab of meat, frozen solid in a little Styrofoam boat covered with plastic.

"How we eat this?" I asked, as the clumpy peas, hard as marbles, rattled into a pan. I was not ready to live in a country where vegetables and meat were sucked like ice cubes.

"Oh, the peas will cook in no time," Erma said, adding water and flipping on her stove's magic, matchless flame. "The round steak we'll have tomorrow. I'll just defrost it in the fridge."

Why not go to the market and get what you want before you eat it? Maybe that was why Americans had to invent frozen food, so they would have something to put in their expensive freezers. Little by little, I was beginning to understand capitalism.

We sat down for my first American dinner, and I shyly waited to see what everyone else did first. I knew some Americans said prayers for their food, perhaps to honor the dead animal they were about to eat, but this seemed like a silly custom. There was a time for praying and a time for eating. Did those same people say prayers when they did other ordinary things—when they made love or went shopping or relieved themselves? I just didn't understand their reasoning, particularly since Americans didn't seem like a particularly spiritual people. Their houses lacked shrines for their ancestors where prayers were said. Anyway, I was happy to see the Munros reach for the food all at once— "digging in," as Leatha called it—like an Oriental family, as soon as we sat down.

My next hurdle was faking the use of their cumbersome eating utensils. In Vietnam, all food was taken with chopsticks or slurped from a bowl. Here, Americans employed as many utensils as the cook had used to prepare the meal. I was sure I'd never master them all, particularly the fork, which everyone held like a pencil, then juggled like acrobats between hands to cut their meat. Why didn't the cook just slice the food into bite-sized strips the way we did in the Orient? I went along with the game as far as I could, grasping my fork like a club and politely smacking my lips very loudly so that Erma and Leatha would know how I enjoyed the meal—despite the rich sauces that filled me up after two bites. Fortunately, after a few seconds of this, nobody looked at me anymore, and Jimmy and I finished our meal winking and poking each other at the kids' end of the table.

After dinner, I wanted to show my new mother-in-law that I could be a good housewife, so I volunteered to do dishes. At first, I was shocked by all the uneaten food. In Vietnam, we believed that the more food you waste in this life, the hungrier you'll be in the next. Then I remembered the full refrigerator and guessed that if people rationed their food as we did in Vietnam, all the freezers and makers would be out of business and go hungry; so, in America, waste was really thrift. I began scraping the plates into the garbage can, and, predictably, Ed came up behind me and laughed his amused-daddy laugh.

"No, no," he said. "Dump the garbage into the sink."

"What?" I knew he must be kidding. "You want to clog drain?" I might be new to America, but I wasn't born yesterday.

"It won't get stopped up. Go ahead. Just dump it down the drain. I'll show you some magic."

I peevishly did as he instructed. *Okay, Mister Smart Man, if you want to play plumber after your supper, that's okay with me!*

When a heap of leavings blocked the drain, I turned on the tap and stood back. Sure enough, the water started to rise. Without blinking an eye, Ed threw a switch over the stove and the pile of sludge became a shaking, squirting volcano, and, miraculously, the pile collapsed and disappeared. The grinding earthquake became a hum and Ed turned off the switch. Tap water ran merrily down the drain.

Pale and humiliated — again — I could only look at the floor. Tears came to my eyes.

"Here now," Ed put his arm around me. "I didn't mean to scare you. That's just a garbage disposal. A motor under the sink grinds everything up."

I took the wrapper the peas came in and started to shove it down the monster's rubbery throat.

"No, no," Ed corrected me again.

I stopped and blew a wisp of hair from my face.

"No paper," Ed warned, "or bones or plastic or anything like that."

"But you say put trash in sink!" This American miracle now seemed a little fickle to be real magic.

"No trash. Just soft food."

Again, I did as I was told, feeling Erma's critical eyes on my back. With the sink now empty, I could at least get on with washing the dishes — something even an ignorant Vietnamese farm girl knew quite well how to do.

"No, no," Ed said when he saw me stacking the dishes in the sink. "Just load them in the dishwasher." He had the same irritating little smile, and I had absolutely no idea whether he was making fun of me or trying to be helpful.

"What you talk about?" I slammed the silverware into the sink. I was getting tired again, and my tone was not properly humble and subservient. I looked over my shoulder into the dining room. Erma and Leatha politely pretended to be absorbed in their coffee and conversation.

"Here—" Ed flipped down the big metal door beside the sink. Inside was a queer wire basket. "Just put the dishes here." He demonstrated with a plate.

"Okay, but how we wash them when they inside?" It seemed a logical question, but it only made Ed laugh. Under his close supervision, I loaded all the dishes in the stupid machine, wondering how even these mechanically inclined Americans got greasy plates and the tines of their silly, useless forks clean without rags and fingers. When I was finished, he poured some powder into a little box on the door and shut it tight. He punched a few buttons and turned a big dial and the growling noise began again. I thought for a minute that the dishes would be ground up, but the whirring was friendlier this time and I could hear the water splashing.

"See?" Ed smiled proudly. "Nothing to it!"

"Okay," I replied, "so how long we wait to dry them?" I fished for a dishtowel.

Ed laughed again. "You don't have to wait. You wipe the counter and go watch TV!"

Okay—I can do that! My first long day in America was coming to an end, and I was ready to accept anything he said at face value. I decided I wouldn't even ask about the machine that put dishes away.

A
NICE
ENGLISH
GIRL

Elizabeth Martinez

efore I met and married Gonzalo, Argentina hardly existed for me, except in relation to the Falklands (or Malvinas) War. Much as I dislike Mrs. Thatcher, a vague picture was imprinted on my mind at that time. Argentineans, it seemed to me, were dark, shadowy creatures with, for some reason, large black mustaches.

I am not myself of true-blue British stock. My mother is Irish and always warned me against marrying a foreigner.

"You'll never feel that his country is your home, and your own country won't be home to you anymore either," she told me. But I didn't heed her advice. I'd always rebelled, although quietly, against the Anglo-Saxon paradise in which I was brought up. I found the rich abundance of the countryside almost suffocating. The heavy sickliness of the scent of wild-flowers in June, blossoming and blooming on every side, tangling through the hedgerows and over the faint pathways, trapped my feet as I walked. The river, which should have been clear, running water, was clogged with rampant blues, yellows, purples, and greens. The poor cows had to quench their thirst between weeds, first breaking their way through a green barrier of branches burgeoning with leaves. The very names of the flowers — knotgrass, hedge bindweed, biting stonecress — expressed encroachment, a desire of the crawling undergrowth to trap and tie together the ancient countryside, too rich and indigestible for my taste.

Such wildness could only be contained by suburban ladies with secateurs, ordering their gardens as they ordered their lives, spending the time between morning coffee and before-dinner drinks snipping and snapping, mercilessly pruning bushes and roses to create gardens of ordered perfection, where no mischievous Robin Goodfellow would dare to tread.

I was never the stuff of which such ladies are made, and although my younger self liked to believe that my marriage sprang from love alone, a pure force guided by the mysterious movements of the stars, I have now come to suspect that one subconscious element in my choice of a spouse was a desire to get away from a crowded island where I never quite felt I belonged.

The umbilical cord with my motherland was not so easily cut, however. Although I left my country, its spirit came with me, and as time goes by, I am confronted with an increasing awareness of the Englishness that is a deeply rooted part of me.

We live in the no-man's-land of Geneva, where practically everyone is a foreigner and people are categorized by their countries. The first thing anyone remarks about me is that I am English. As for myself, whenever I meet an English person, however different from me they may initially seem to be, we always have some slight thing in common, a shared joke, a television program we both once liked, a vague memory of steak-and-kidney pies that came in a tin, or a squirrel puppet that used to show us how to cross the road. With time I have begun to look back on my birthplace with nostalgia. I've even shed secret tears over it. I realize now that I'm not so intent on being an "individual," that I do after all have a national identity.

In many ways I did not know my own Britishness until I visited Gonzalo's family in Argentina. They were waiting for us at the airport with tears streaming down their faces. The warmth of their welcome made me feel extraordinarily stiff and British. When his mother put her arms around me and propelled me out of the terminal, some most unwelcome Anglo-Saxon gene popped into my head and made me feel like saying "Excuse me, madame, but we've only just met. Please control your effusive emotion. Remember that above all I am British."

The motorway that led us home was rimmed with Bolivians selling large butterfly-like kites and by shanty towns. Gonzalo had never mentioned shanty towns to me. His parents obviously found them, and the dark-skinned people who lived in them, an embarrassment, not to be shown to a nice English girl like me.

From that journey onwards I began to see myself through the eyes of my family-in-law and to realize that to them, and probably to most of the rest of the world, I was not a teenage misfit dreaming of escape. I was simply a nice English girl in a flowery dress, too pale to go out in the fierce southern sun, and too naive to so much as go for a walk alone in Buenos Aires. A girl whose main claim to notice was the fact that she had *ojos claros* (blue eyes).

I was no longer the person I had always believed myself to be. I had become a stereotype. I was the daughter of Vera Lynn, the sister of Princess Di, Britannia's shield and Winston Churchill's cigar.

Almost the first thing I saw as I left the airport was an enormous sign saying bluntly, *Las Malvinas son Argentinos* (the Falklands are Argentinean). A few days after our arrival, we were invited to tea in a reputedly rough area of Buenos Aires called *Las Nuces*. The house we visited was very humble, a two-room concrete box with walls painted the blue color one finds the Third

World over, decorated by pictures cut from magazines. Our hostess was a mestizo from Tucaman in the north of Argentina, and the soul of hospitality.

Virtually the whole neighborhood popped in at one time or another, curious to see her English visitor no doubt. One man believed that I was Australian. When Gonzalo informed him that I was English, he made an expression of mock (I hope) horror and drew a finger across his throat with a ghastly murderous hiss, indicating, I presume, that he wished to slit my gullet from ear to ear. At that time diplomatic relations between England and Argentina had only just been resumed, and memories of war were fresh. I wanted to say to him, "But you can have the Falklands, I don't care who has them and can't bear Mrs. Thatcher."

But I couldn't say anything, couldn't by any means make an appropriate joke. My Spanish was rudimentary, and I knew that the best thing to do was merely to smile politely as I sipped my coffee, to remain anonymous, diplomatic, noncommittal—polite and, above all, British. After all, that was what they wanted me to be. Nobody in Argentina wanted to know who I really was. They wanted me to be the archetypal English daughter-in-law. The representative of a country that had introduced trains, scones, and silver tea services to Argentina. In meeting me, they wanted to grow closer to the land of pomp and circumstance—a place they imagined to be entirely populated by men in plus fours and ladies in floaty dresses and large hats preparing cucumber sandwiches—where they believed life would be like a leisurely row down a tranquil river. They did not want me to express myself, they wanted me to reflect the sparkle of the crown jewels and bring them a breath of the soft and balmy isle they believed England to be.

On the same day as our visit to Las Nuces, we went for a barbecue at "Uncle George's house." This was altogether a surrealistic evening. George is a "character," and because I spoke very little Spanish, he decided to communicate with me in Italian, a language that neither of us spoke a word of. His Italian consisted of hysterical Spanish with an *o* on the end of all the words, so that, for example, he called himself "Georgio." This farce continued for more than two hours, during which time I grinned politely and so steadily that I thought my cheeks were seizing up. "Keka"—Gonzalo's granny—was so furious at this exhibition in front of an honored guest that she would not speak to George for several days afterward. All this took place as I was presented with various barbecued objects from the inside of a cow, parts I would never have imagined people actually ate. One of the most repulsive was the cow's tonsils, which looked rather like a large, white, gristly raspberry. My first literal taste of unadulterated Argentina revealed my own conservatism to me.

After Las Nuces, I began to resent the way people stereotyped me. All the intricacies of my personality, the embroidery of my far-from-perfect character, the holes and insufficiencies that make me who I am, just as holes make up the delicacy of lace, were wiped out by my overwhelming presence as British. The Argentineans saw somebody calm, dignified, respectable, nice, but not really me.

It was not until my second trip to Argentina that I began to come to terms with these stereotypes. During this trip, my husband and I ventured further into the interior of the country. We went to the little white house in the woods where Gonzalo had spent all of his childhood days. The house is what may with justice be called an idyllic place, two miles from a village where the main means of transport remains horseback. It hides in dark, shimmering woods between endless empty mountains and a deserted rocky river that, usually gentle, swells with force after the rains.

The little house has no electricity and a mere trickle of water in its pipes. It has thick and stony walls, decorated with damp, and an undulating earthen floor. The kitchen smells faintly of old cooking. Its walls are blackened, and a mere patch of light enters through the small square window that squints out onto woods inhabited by giant toads that could squirt you in the eye and blind you and beetles that could bite you just below the eye, injecting a poison that takes thirty painful years to kill you.

But when the sun is high, streaming yellow through the shadows, the place is perfect. As one walks to the river through the silky grass, hosts of glistening insects rise up with each step. Their humming is constant, both night and day, interspersed with the cackling of clouds of green parakeets that drift from tree to tree like errant scarves, and the distant call of what could be a puma.

We were away from civilization and among the people of the provinces, who laugh at the arrogant *porteños* of Buenos Aires. Imagine, then, how an English girl appeared to them. On our first night in the village, we ate in a small cafe, a totally plain room painted blue and decorated with pictures of the deified Argentinean football team. In the middle of the ceiling, there was a neon lamp beneath which we sat, and around which a horde of the most extraordinary surrealistic insects hovered. By some amazing trick, these insects managed to fall into the middle of my pizza — nobody else's, just mine. As each successive clown-painted acrobat dived into my cheese, I sprang back from the table in fright and caused my family-in-law, who merely picked the insects up by their garish wings and cast them down to the floor, to laugh at my horror. I had always thought of myself as a great lover of nature, but there was rather too much nature for me in Córdoba, certainly too much of it in my pizza. Although I wore jeans and tennis shoes, I suddenly felt as though I were wearing a very prim navy suit and high-heeled shoes, and perhaps horn-rimmed glasses. I saw myself as my family-in-law saw me, and I felt more comfortable with this vision than I had before.

In fact, on our last evening in Córdoba, my husband wanted me to embody that image more completely. We were invited to Auntie Christina's house, and my husband told me that I should dress up. I objected because, as far as I could see, nobody in the village ever wore anything more respectable than jeans. "But you are English," he insisted, so I obediently changed. So there I was, sitting in the shadowy candlelit living room beneath the moth-eaten skin of a puma some family member had once shot, wearing a red Laura Ashley dress and pearls — an exotic, incongruous creature in the midst of the family in their ragged shorts and jeans. One of the cousins played folk songs on his guitar, and the other members of the family sang. All evening long, they swayed and sighed, smiling and reminiscing.

I could not join in their songs, but sitting there quietly in my English outfit, I made them happy and, in a strange way, became one of them. Ironically, I could become part of my Argentinean family by becoming what they wanted me to be, by assuming my Englishness. I came to see my nationality as a costume assigned to me by destiny. I have little choice but to cover my spirit with it and try to appreciate it as my Argentinean family appreciates it.

THE WEIGHT OF WATER: BEARING A WOMAN'S BURDEN

Faith Eidse

n many girlhood mornings I woke to the image of brown sinewy women struggling out of a Zairian river valley, wading through a fog coverlet, bearing loads of firewood and manioc tubers on their heads.

By the time the sun rose full in their angular faces, they had hoed their manioc fields, chopped firewood, and retrieved a load of soaking manioc from the riverbed. The waterlogged tuber was thus leached of arsenic but weighed up to fifty pounds as the wiry women labored beneath it a mile uphill. A metaphor for the women's bitter portion, the tuber was laid on drying racks in the sun and left to bake while the women hurried back to the river, in the noonday furnace, for the day's supply of water. When they returned, spinal columns pressed beneath ten-gallon buckets, they set the water down, trying not to spill a drop, and returned to dinner preparations. They sliced thick, barklike peels off the manioc, cut it into bite-sized pieces and pounded it into a fine flour. They heaved hardwood pestles the size of their own thighs into mortars to rhythmic grunts, "uh-huh-unh, uh-huh-unh." The flour was then sifted and pounded again, until it could be mixed with boiling water into a sticky ball of opaque mush. I watched an evening meal prepared in under twelve hours, not counting the tilling, seeding, weeding, harvest, and soak cycles.

I felt these women could survive anything—wind, water, heat, childbirth, child death. Their backs were often clutched by infants secured by wrappers, as they pounded, hoed, or strained forward beneath creaking handwoven baskets or shining pails. One even bore on her shoulders and breasts the teeth marks of a crocodile that had gripped her in a death roll, unable to defeat her in its subaquatic world.

I followed these women to the river from the time I was eight years old. While Mother dispensed drugs at the clinic and Dad translated the Bible, my sisters and I let the village raise us. We raced and slid after the Kamayala women, down steep, gullied paths, shadow balls bouncing along under the midday sun, amid their Chokwe banter. They laughed at us for wearing slips into the river ("Take them off!") and for coming all the way without a container for water.

I soon learned to wind a tight headpad from a square cloth and balance a two-gallon gourd, no hands. My head was a pendulum moving counter to the slosh, as I followed the water uphill. The path rose a mile out of the jungle floor, and the water grew heavier as we climbed, my neck crushed into my collarbones. I planted each step deliberately, weaving back and forth across gullies, and gave myself to the distracting banter of our village friends.

I learned as a child that women's work lasts all day. They work at menial labor because they are women and because colonialists selected men to be educated and employed. A market economy further devalued their survival labor, creating what a Ghanaian friend says is not double but triple oppression. The muscle-bound women of Africa are unpaid laborers for a male elite. It is their strength and know-how that helps them survive, but it also allows men a more intellectual pursuit. This is the perception of postcolonial African writers, such as Tsitsi Dangarembga, who fled her patriarchal culture and, for a time, her native Zimbabwe. It was also my discovery, well into a womanhood I had modeled on the weight-bearing African woman.

In this I was inadvertently following my own grandmothers, pioneers of the Manitoba prairie who made their own soap, laundered knuckle-to-washboard, mended by lamplight, kneaded *zwiebach*, rolled piecrust, picked acres of raspberries until their knuckles were stained with their own blood. Like the women of the newly independent African nations (I was five years old when Zaire, the country of my birth, gained its independence), they were the economic backbone of a new country, the sustainers of several generations. While my grandpas built roads and farms, my grandmas worked in the margins, their labor considered secondary, their roles taken for granted.

The mother in Dangarembga's *Nervous Conditions* explains the weight of womanhood to her daughter, Tambu, then eight. The speech is familiar to women worldwide who learned that a woman's lot is self-sacrifice:

"This business of womanhood is a heavy burden," she said. "How could it not be? Aren't we the ones who bear children? When it is like that you can't just decide today I want to do this, tomorrow I want to do that, the next day I want to be educated! When there are sacrifices to be made, you are the one who has to make them. And these things are not easy; you have to start learning them early from a very early age. The earlier the better so that it is easy later on. Easy! As if it is ever easy. And these days it is worse, with the poverty of blackness on one side and the weight of womanhood on the other. Aiwa! What will help you, my child, is to learn to carry your burdens with strength."

The mother's speech is a turning point for the young Tambu. She does not want to be impoverished or burdened. She wants education, but her father is angry when she announces it. He's "thinking that I expected him to obtain the money somehow, perhaps by working." Dangarembga's view is that men are elitist, even lazy, and that victimization of women is everywhere men are, in the village or the mission center, learned or unlearned, rich or poor. When Tambu asks for seed to grow her own maize for school fees, her father is derisive.

Tambu's rebellion comes early — at age eight, when she still has a sense of self — and is spurred by contempt for her brother, who gets school admission handed to him despite his laziness. Only when her brother dies of the mumps is education handed to her. All her manual labor — cultivating and hoeing maize to earn her education — is slavery compared to the support the family is willing to give when no male alternative exists.

Judging from my girlhood and adolescence among the Chokwe-Lunda people of Zaire, Dangarembga is being brutally honest about the sexist echelons of her Shona tribe in Zimbabwe. During a typical lunch hour, while I was a girl at Kamayala, the men were moving their chairs a second time into the receding shade as the women returned from a second trip to the river. Dangarembga doesn't characterize all men so harshly. But even those who are willing to work hard benefit from first-class status.

My friend Kafi from neighboring Kahemba, Zaire, niece of a prosperous merchant, told me recently of her visit home between graduate courses in Canada. The men of her family and she, the honored guest, were seated at a table set with glasses and a new African beer. She uncapped a bottle, poured herself a drink, and praised it. But the men waited. "Who will pour our drinks?" said one. Kafi knew they expected her to, since she was a woman and, therefore, beneath them. But she had her drink and didn't see why they couldn't pour their own. She continued sipping and remarking on its robust flavor. "We need a woman to pour our drinks," another man said. Kafi's cousin, sitting nearby, painting her nails, caught on to Kafi's protest and also refused to pour the drinks. Finally, the men called a servant girl, less than twelve years old, from dinner preparations in the kitchen to pour their drinks.

I was imprinted by a pan-cultural patriarchy, raised as I was in a traditional Mennonite home. Daddy was privileged in our family, permitted to read while the table was set and dinner served. His four daughters were not permitted to read until all the domestic chores were done. But Dad was also full of good will, serenading us on Hawaiian guitar at bedtime if mother had to retire early with a headache. He funded several promising Kamayala men through medical and education doctorates overseas, so that I quietly buried my own hopes of entering a major university. We girls were sent to Bible College and were expected to marry for status.

My choice was an aspiring American scientist, a man whose voice, metaphorically speaking, would resonate from the shade at the village center. I settled into a support position in the marriage, never questioning my secondary role until twelve years later, when I found myself catatonically depressed. Tears flowed unbidden, and my then two-year-old son crawled up on my lap, pressed himself close, and cried along with me.

Early in our marriage, while my American husband began his doctoral research, I slipped easily into the working woman mode, slogging day and night as a cub reporter at the *Virginia Gazette*, earning minimum wage. I covered courts, crime, and city government during the week; varsity sports and features, evenings and weekends. It was not unusual for me to have fourteen or fifteen bylines a week. I paused long enough to do the laundry or throw together bag lunches and skillet dinners.

Only when I'd given up my job to help my husband type his dissertation and prepare for his oral defense, only when I'd stayed up three nights running, driven to bitter anxiety by his deadline, did I begin to sense the self-betrayal I labored under. At his thesis party, I was fed the old saw—the one Gloria Steinem had already debunked—"His degree is half yours."

I accepted graciously. "It better be," I said, but recognized the lie. His friends had reinforced my role as helpmate, excused me for having no overarching pursuit of my own. I saw that his degree wasn't mine at all. I had nothing to show for all the hours I'd put in. Like that of my African sisters, my work was invisible. I barely had a profession since I had pursued no advanced degree, and certainly no chance at being hired at a salary equal to my husband's. I realized, as Tambu did, that I wanted more. More learning, more time to read and study. But whenever I cracked a book, some duty invaded, a sinkful of dishes, a load of laundry. I tried to shut it out, but I couldn't concentrate until the chore was done. And my chores were about to triple.

I never let on to my husband that carrying an eight-pound baby to term was anything more than normal wear and tear. I was a woman, hardened on the African savanna, strengthened by the weight of water, inured to the back-breaking work of survival, devoted to the cycles of life. Except for my dragging feet during weekend hikes from Somerville to Harvard Square, and my penchant for falling asleep in my dinner plate, he might not have noticed any change in my daily pace.

At work, before the baby came, I had been honored with a load increase, so that I was putting out supplements for twelve weekly papers and one daily, in addition to my regular weekend magazine. As I ballooned and my feet overflowed my shoes, people were constantly telling me to sit down, put my feet up. "But wait! Don't move that chair! In your condition! Call a reporter. Let the guys do the heavy lifting."

I was impatient with their genteel attitude. Give me a pail of water, a hill to climb. I could meet deadline three trimesters pregnant on my hands and knees. I continued running stairs, climbing furniture to get at storage shelves, racing to meet press runs, while my assistant gaped and begged to take some of the load.

"Ha," I scoffed inwardly, "wimpy Americans. I am Muscle Mama, raised on Zairian survivalism. I can carry gallons of water in the scalding midday sun."

I balked at giving up control, but I couldn't keep up the pace I'd set for myself. One morning, while running for the train at Porter Square and hauling a seam-cracking briefcase, I jounced an inner-thigh nerve to numbness. When I got to work, I couldn't walk. I called the doctor, who assured me it was temporary, and so I scooted around the building all day in my office chair.

"We don't need your salary," my husband said, and for $15,000 a year, I didn't argue. Besides, my make-do, bake-from-scratch, more-with-less wizardry meant we could live on his $20,000 postdoctoral stipend until he got a full-salary job.

I handed in my notice and prepared to seal myself into my nest like the ground hornbill of Africa. The large black and yellow birds make mud from their own dung to seal the female inside a hollow tree trunk. They leave only a slit for her large, casqued beak, so the male can feed her while she incubates their young. When all the eggs are hatched, the mother may break her way out, but she's been known to get stuck in the process, unable to move either backward or forward.

My birthing was cushy compared to that of African women who've delivered roadside while hauling loads of water or firewood. I had a husband massaging me through twelve hours of back labor, and the nursing staff on hand at Emerson Hospital, Concord. Yet I felt as though I was standing still in the middle of the Concord Pike at rush hour with a semi bearing down on me. The contractions felt like a two-ton tractor-trailer colliding with my lower back, backing up, gunning its engines and careening into me again. Alternately, I prayed, "Oh God," and cursed, "Oooh Gawd," until my prayer became a curse and my curse became a prayer. My husband was alarmed that a woman in her most sanctified hour (hadn't the Apostle Paul promised we'd be saved in childbirth?) could sound so heathen and tried to shush me. "Look at me," he commanded. "Breathe with me." But when transition hit, piling semi upon semi, I shut him out completely. I didn't want him to touch or talk to me. I didn't want to push through; I only wanted to push back and away or

be mercifully annihilated. But my body kept right on working despite my resistance. It was the model of endurance the
Chokwe women had seemed to promise it would be. I didn't
tear worth a stitch during delivery, and my baby, placed wailing
on my belly, climbed my slippery body and rooted on contact,
his gums clamping a firm nipple.

Breast-feeding was such a natural reflex after seeing it as part
of the rhythm of work in Zaire that a prenatal nurse was horrified when she caught me breast-feeding and talking on the
phone at the same time. "You're not watching the clock," she
said, releasing my baby's suction and pulling him off me.
"You're not timing the baby evenly on both sides. How would
you like to end up with lopsided breasts?"

I wondered at her authority to interfere with my succoring,
and at how she, an obstetrical nurse, could view breasts in the
dominant male way, as form not function. In Zaire, lactating
women bared their breasts obliviously and fed each other's children, much as Americans share sodas.

Within two days I was released from the hospital and was
back in the kitchen. The first thing I did was turn on a burner,
heat up a homemade chicken potpie (cooked before I'd entered
the hospital), and set the table. Then I quietly locked myself in
the bathroom and sat on the tub. From somewhere deep inside,
a geyser opened, a gush from a subterranean cavern, so full, so
bottomless, so dark and bitter, I could not stop its rush. How
could I take care of this baby all by myself? How could I keep
him from dragging me under, his gum marks already imprinted
on my breasts? I had permitted one man's needs to supersede my
own, and now I was giving all that was left to this hungry child.
I sobbed for the sisterhood of the village, for a group of women
who shared the weight of babies and water.

My husband had not yet held or touched the baby. I had
tried to trick him into it, had pretended, for a change, that I
wasn't all Zairian Mama. I had asked him, please, to carry the
baby in from the car. Instead he had unbuckled the entire infant
seat and carried the whole thing in as a unit, even though we

had an infant seat waiting in the apartment. He had set it on the floor, in my domain, as if to say, "Here's your baby and car seat, what's for dinner?"

It seemed in that moment, on the tub, I could view the shape of my life, and it was a dark narrow hole. The tasks of bonding, childcare, imprinting would be born by me alone. I was stuck in my hole well into the monolithic year two-thousand-and-one, the year my new baby would get his driver's license.

Less than a year later, home in Canada to show off my toddling boy, I rattled on as though I hadn't talked to anyone in a year. My mother stopped me in midsentence.

"Did you hear what you just said?" she asked.

"What?"

"You said, 'Ever since I became a single mother . . .'"

By then my husband had held his son, had tickled his toes, had tossed him in the air. He had spent five to ten minutes most days after work playing with our child. Meanwhile, my schedule had become dictated by the baby, sculpted by his feedings, diaperings, baths, climbing, and naps. During cold spells the two of us were shut into a gray apartment for days on end. The budget needed my freelance-writing income, but I found it difficult to get my research done. Babysitting exchanges with other mothers worked, except that the trade-offs doubled the babies I had to watch and tripled my need to get out.

Perhaps I was standing in my own way, afraid of success. Maybe if I was able to release my child to someone else's care, I could reenter the marketplace — provided I didn't have to carry the full load at home, too. I raised the issue with my husband. "What if I returned to work, would you share the second shift with me?"

"Why should I?" he asked. He had the high-wage job. See how he supported my writing hobby, how hard he worked every day to provide for us?

In my willingness to take over the household drudgery, to wash every dish, every day of our marriage, I had unwittingly installed the elitist male of my girlhood. I had revived the Chokwe symbol of beauty — a line of young men strolling along a palm-lined avenue, shirts open to their navels, examining their inch-long fingernails, glancing sidelong at a group of women bearing water from the river, hoping for approval.

But survivor that I was, the African savanna burned on my retina, I shouldered on, eventually adding a second son to the lineup. I kissed my boys and told them they were beautiful. I served them and bathed them and tucked them to bed, running for a last glass of water, lingering to tell one more African tale.

Through my children, I found women to commiserate with, how to stretch a dollar, how to clothe a family on a single salary in high-rent Boston. There were international wives like myself, from Vancouver, Zurich, Cologne. Some of them had no choice, no working visas. That was okay. Weren't we at-home mothers central to society?

It took a family upheaval to show me the fault of that myth. When we moved from the Boston suburbs to Florida in summer 1992, the scalding sand underfoot, the palms dry and crackling in the smothering heat, transported me to the Africa of my girlhood and recalled the strong women I'd followed to the river.

But as the days and weeks passed, I found myself shut in from the blistering heat with a two-year-old and no friends to talk to. I had given up my mobility, telling my husband he could have the car for work. I had intended to volunteer at my elder son's school, had intended to join university clubs, had intended to revise my novel, but I found I didn't have the means or the energy. Outside my windows the birds sang, but I was deaf to their muffled chirps. The kudzu bloomed around my back door infusing the apartment with the artificial sweet smell of death, reminding me of a corpse lying in a village beyond the Kamayala leprosarium, a man dead after a long illness. His widow was shunted to a mourning hut, a mere pup tent made of pitched sticks and covered by a dark cloth wrapper.

There she sat, shorn of her proper clothing, dignity, and status, while the in-laws cleaned her house of its possessions. For three days she sat, cramped in a hut the size of a broom closet.

She would sit four days, if her suffering didn't overwhelm her, to prove that she was a daughter-in-law worthy of service to her in-laws, and to show the respect due her husband. When she emerged, she would be more beholden than ever to her husband's clan, "a thing of service," wrote Mariama Bâ in her book, *So Long a Letter.*

Bâ wrote of her own suffering as a pioneering feminist in Senegal. Her story concerns a polygamous marriage, in which a first wife, Ramatoulaye, is tossed aside for a second. The second wife is young and pretty, the age of Ramatoulaye's daughter. Ramatoulaye gains strength from challenging the Islamic lie of equal sharing among wives. (She never again gets a chance to converse with her husband after he sneaks to his second wedding without a word to her.) After her husband's death and a stint with the second wife in a mourning tent, Ramatoulaye gains courage by standing up to men who assume she will capitulate to any marriage offer, even if it's to become the spoiling second wife. She gains freedom by depending on the friendship of a radicalized woman, Aissatou, who has left her own polygamous marriage. Bâ recognizes that it is men who make themselves central to traditional society. They formulate and hand down the laws, happy to point to token women legislators whose numbers are far below equal representation.

Women are pushed to the periphery, pushed further still when they have children. A woman's status is endangered by age and childbearing, as when Ramatoulaye is thrown over for a younger woman, or when she learns that her coed daughter is pregnant and may be expelled from university. The boyfriend remains "flat," never unwillingly burdened or punished for impregnating her daughter.

Because Bâ derives optimism, as many women do, from raising children, she characterizes Ramatoulaye's sons-in-law as new men, willing to share in childcare and cooking. But what the modern woman realizes is that if she doesn't enter into a relationship on equal footing, if she marries for status, instead of by understood equal contract, she will have to struggle for every liberty she gains. And most often that struggle will have to begin with admission of her own self-betrayal.

So it was with me, the Nugrape smell of kudzu heavy in the air. Huddled in a tent the size of a fist, mourning the loss of my self-worth, seeing my negation for the first time, I had to admit how much of the traditional myth—African and universal—I had bought wholesale. I had believed that if I accepted my place, and the drudgery of domestic servitude, I could earn a happy home. I had believed that if I stayed home, chained to the stove, my boys would grow up well adjusted and healthy.

Amid the muffled birdsong, I detected the crack in that logic from an event four years earlier. I had noticed my elder son, then four, struggling with his three-year-old girl cousin. They were playing in the motor home we'd traveled in to Canada. My son was pushing at the metal door, trying to keep his cousin inside.

"You stay home with the baby," he spluttered. "I'm going to work."

His cousin puffed out her plump cheeks and turned crimson. "No, I'm going to work! You stay home with the baby."

Finally, impressed by her vehemence, my son let her out and they both went off to work, leaving the baby home alone.

Not only was I demanding too little for my life, but, by accepting second-class citizenship for myself, I was teaching my sons to be chauvinists.

For six months I listened to therapists tell me I was capable, intelligent, worthy. I was worth an education, I was worth a career, I was worth hiring someone to take care of my children for me, I was worth admission to a major university, one with a solid creative writing program. More than that, it had become the only way to survive.

Bâ and Dangarembga, too, see education as the African woman's hope for equality. But it should be an education with eyes open, minds critical of traditional oppression. Women's burdens should increasingly be those of books and learning. Women's "sacred mission," Bâ wrote, should be to strike out "at the archaic practices, traditions and customs that are not a real part of our precious cultural heritage."

Part of that heritage, the part that has made me willing to improve my status in my intercultural marriage, is the strength and survival of African women who struggle under some of the harshest conditions known to womankind.

In recent months, as I burrowed into my thesis novel, my husband showed a remarkable tolerance for neglected housework. I overheard him tell a guest, "I would like the house to be neater, but I don't say anything."

Said she: "Why don't you clean it yourself?"

ANOTHER TRADITIONAL ARAB-JEWISH IOWA POTLUCK

Fern Kupfer

icture this: My new husband and I are in Florida at a party for my parents' fiftieth wedding anniversary. In celebration of this achievement, my parents are flying to Israel in a few days. Their lifelong friends are all at this party: Sylvia and Harold, Leon and Carl, Bernice and Harry. They are talking with great enthusiasm about Israel, about the trips that they have all taken; one couple has even attended a grandson's bar mitzvah in the promised land.

My husband enters the conversation, an innocent. He says how he would *love* to go to Israel someday, that he was so sorry not to have been able to visit when he was in the Middle East in the early seventies. "I was in Egypt, in Syria, in Lebanon for a few weeks . . . ," Joe goes on.

My parents' friends look puzzled. How could anyone go to the Middle East and not make Israel the prime destination? "So close and you didn't get to Israel?" someone asks.

"Well, Joe's not Jewish," I tell my parents' friends, gently letting them know that Israel doesn't quite have the same meaning for him. There is the assumption that because he is my husband, because he is short and dark and looks, in fact, like a lot of the other men in the room, that Joe is Jewish.

"Well, I wanted to go to Israel," my husband says. "But I couldn't."

My parents' friends are attentive. I hold my breath. "You *couldn't?*" someone finally responds. Now everyone looks totally confused.

My husband goes on to explain that because he was *born* in Lebanon there was a problem. "You see, my passport was limited . . . ," he continues.

It doesn't matter. A hush falls around the room as I watch the click-click of each face when the sudden recognition hits: the recognition that not only has Ruth and Milton's daughter married a non-Jew, but she has actually gone and married one of *them*. That the short, dark man before them is — yes, he really is — an *Arab*!

I suggested that on the wedding invitations we should put: "What? Another Traditional Arab-Jewish Iowa Potluck?" It was a second marriage for both of us, and there should have been lots of shaky ground. Different religions, different cultural backgrounds, and yes, the children. Right before Joe and I married, my mother sent me an article about blended families. Studies showed that ten and thirteen were the most difficult ages for children to adjust to a second marriage. Ten and thirteen. The exact ages of the daughters who lived full time with my soon-to-be. Thanks, Mom, I said. My own daughter was just off to college. My son, Zachariah, severely handicapped since birth, was living in a children's facility about forty minutes away.

My mother *didn't* say anything about Joe's not being Jewish. Better still, she didn't say anything about his being an Arab (not to me and certainly not to any of her friends). But what did my family know of Arabs? There were only images of *them*—often as enemies of Israel, as terrorists. No distinctions were made. The Syrians, the Saudis, the Lebanese; the Muslims, the Christians, the Melkites, the Shiites, the Copts—all blended together into this monolithic group. Arabs were *them*: a swarthy, untrustworthy, rock-throwing people; the enemies of Israel. Arabs were who killed the Israeli athletes in Munich. Arabs were who threw grenades into busloads of school children. Try it as a word association among Jews. "Arab—fill in the blank." The following word is often "terrorist."

The summer before Joe and I were married, he took me to Toledo, Ohio, to meet his family. His sister Geni put out a lavish spread with all the traditional Lebanese foods. His brother and his wife were there, his mother, and his Aunt Odette, who was visiting from Egypt and spoke no English. I sat with my daughter at the table, eating with our fingers the spicy eggplant rolled in pita, the stuffed grape leaves, and listening to the lively conversation in Arabic. I whispered in my daughter's ear: "What are two nice Jewish girls doing in a place like this?"

What we were doing, of course, was sharing food and family stories, the same as both our peoples had done for centuries. And what struck me again and again as I learned about my husband's family—their history, their values—was how very *similar* it all was to my own and how the cultures crossed more smoothly than anyone would imagine.

Joe and I were both over forty when we married, and we both are writers and professors of English at Iowa State University. Both of us, too, had lived through some hard times. To say that in middle age we came into this new relationship with old baggage is an understatement. We came packed with steamer trunks—just the way Joe came into this country in the first place.

My husband, Joseph Geha, was born in 1944, in Zahle, Lebanon, a mountain town high above the Bekaa valley, halfway between Damascus and Beirut. After World War II, his father packed up a young wife and three children and came to America, where they lived above the grocery store that he opened in Toledo with money saved from years of peddling dry goods.

Joe didn't speak English until the first grade, where he was teased for his accent, called "dirty A-rab," and embarrassed for the strange foods his mother put in his lunchbox — the leftover ground cinnamon lamb, the sweet greens cooked down in olive oil and garlic and rolled into paper-thin *lawash* bread. He insisted that he no longer be called "Zuzu" — the Arabic diminutive for Yousef — but "Joe," a solidly American name. Oh, how he longed to be American. To eat peanut butter and jelly on Wonder Bread. To have parents who understood things like cub scouts and baseball and PTA.

Keenly, all through his childhood and adolescence, he felt the difference. And even though he was the first in his family to graduate from college — and went on to become a writer and a college professor himself — the difference, the sense of himself as an outsider, I think, remains with him today. (Though he has come to appreciate his roots now — certainly his culinary ones. I eat with enthusiasm the foods of my husband's childhood, the food he makes with recipes handed down from all the women in his family. Once we got a package in the mail, the brown wrapper dripping with honey: baklava from Aunt Sophie in Detroit. There was no accompanying note. Aunt Sophie can cook but she cannot write. In our spice cabinet there is a homemade mix: Aunt Maheeba's special blend of cumin and cinnamon and coriander. And last year, when Joe visited his mother as she lay dying in a Toledo hospital, he brought her *sfeeha*, traditional spinach and feta pies, which he had made from her recipe. Among her last words to him before her death were: "Next time, more lemon.")

I, too, come from an immigrant background, but the third generation distanced me from the Old World, a world of such bitter anti-Semitism and poverty that my grandfather gave thanks every day for living in America. I remember Papa petting Cleo, our family dog: "To be in America, even a dog is lucky," he would tell us.

I was born in the Bronx and lived in a neighborhood called the Amalgamated, cooperative housing built in the early part of this century by immigrant Jews, many of whom had socialist affiliations — ergo, the name "The Amalgamated," from "The Amalgamated Workers Union." My mother grew up there, married, and after I was born in 1946, lived with my father in a large sunny apartment shared with my grandparents and my Aunt Anna who took the subway every day to her secretarial job in the city. For a number of years, I was the only, doted-upon child among all these adults. I had a happy childhood with someone always available to read to me or rub my back until I fell asleep. Later, I recall reading scary Nancy Drew mysteries at night and asking my Papa to come sit in my room to "watch me read," a request he never seemed to think at all unusual.

Of course we were Jewish. The butcher, the baker, every neighbor and friend in that Bronx neighborhood was Jewish. So there was not the sense that being Jewish was in any way different — something I only experienced when I was an adult, living in Iowa. Where I grew up, everyone was Jewish. The schools were closed for Jewish holidays, and Christmas only meant that downtown department stores were decorated with trees and tinsel.

Once, in the early fifties, my family went to upstate New York on a vacation with some friends, the Cohens. My family had reserved a room in this fancy hotel, but when the Cohens arrived, the rooms were mysteriously all taken (my family did not have a "Jewish" last name, so our reservations had been accepted). I remember my father coming back to the car, furious: "The place is restricted," he told my mother. When she told me what "restricted" meant, I was totally puzzled. Why would anyone not want to rent a hotel room to Jews? And if they didn't let Jews in, how in the world could they find enough people to stay in business?

For me, like a lot of New Yorkers of my generation, being Jewish was an ethnic rather than a religious identity. My family did not go to synagogue—in fact, because of their socialist leanings, they did not accept the traditions of religious Jews. No one kept kosher. I did not go to Hebrew school. Jewish holidays such as Passover and Rosh Hashana (the Jewish New Year) were celebrated as family gatherings rather than religious holidays. My brother did not have a Bar Mitzvah (unusual for my parents' generation even among the most secular of Jews).

And yet, I was Jewish. I never felt anything but. This deep-rooted ethnic and historical identity came from living with immigrant Jewish grandparents who spoke Yiddish in our home, whose values about education and family and ways of being in the world were connected to what I understood as "Jewishness."

There was a certain chauvinism about this. My grandfather always had books about famous Jews and Jews who *should* have been famous had they received the recognition they deserved from the gentile world of power. My grandfather had theories about who *really* invented the telephone and discovered America and cured diseases—every one a Jew. It was implied in my family that there were certain ways of behaving. Jewish children didn't get bad grades in school, Jewish women didn't keep sloppy homes, Jewish husbands didn't go to bars or hit their wives. People who were not good with money had *goyisha kops* (gentile heads). Jews respected bookishness and were clearly unenamored of the American fascination with football, guns, and motorcycles. Comedian Lenny Bruce used to have a routine in which he made the distinctions between goyish and Jewish: trailer parks and lime jello and the Marine Corps are goyish; condos and rye bread and accounting are Jewish; everyone in the Midwest is gentile, even if they're not; everyone in New York is Jewish, even if they're not. Especially Italians. Italians are very Jewish, Bruce said.

And so, I might add, are Arabs. Which is why Joe and I seem so at home in each other's skin. As if we come from the same place. To illustrate, here's another story with my parents in

Florida: Joe is in the bathroom, but the door is open, and he is rummaging through the medicine cabinet to look for his sinus medication. From the hall, I hear him and ask if he's looking for aspirin. "No," he calls back. "I'm just taking one of these." In the doorway, he shakes his prescription bottle.

"What's he taking?" calls my mother from the kitchen. "He's taking a pill?"

My father yells in from the bedroom: "Is he sick? What's the matter with him?" (If my grandparents were still alive, they would be calling, too, from their respective places in the house.) My husband looks at me, smiling.

"I feel like I'm back on Monroe Street," he says. Monroe Street, where he lived with his family above the store.

My husband and I both come from a place where parents are in the habit of intensely observing their children, where it is not possible to come into a room without having one's appearance commented upon. A belt improperly looped. A stooped shoulder. A pimple on the forehead. All were fodder for interpretation and advice. A forehead would not be broken out if bangs were pulled away from a face. Too much sun is dangerous, but a little color couldn't hurt. And all behavior is open to public scrutiny: "What's he taking that pill for, anyway?"

It's the intrusiveness, I think. A kind of well-meaning busybodiness that characterized both our homes and separated us from the more emotionally remote families — the ones my family called *goyisha*, what Joe's referred to as *Amerkani*.

And the talk, too. My husband and I both come from storytelling families. Lots of time spent around the kitchen table talking about this one and that one, examining every nuance of intimate relationships, mixing memory and desire so the stories became richer and more complex over time. There was the story of my grandmother coming to America by herself at age sixteen, fleeing her own domineering mother and an arranged marriage. ("I took one look at him standing there under the town clock and I said to my mother: '*You* marry him! I am going to America!'") There was the story of my grandfather, who had seen the Czar, who came to America with seventy-five cents in his pocket: "And I did not speak von vord of English, not von vord!" He used to make a fist and pound it on the table as if to emphasize the peril.

My husband remembers the Sundays with family in Toledo: "All talk, only talk. No television, no ball games. Just talk over Turkish coffee, men with cigars after dinner telling stories, women reading the grounds in their cups and laughing. And everyone talking."

When I was ten years old, my family moved to suburban Long Island—next to Israel, the promised land for my parents' generation. What used to be potato fields became a development of identical split-level homes with streets named "Deborah Drive" and "Judith Avenue." (Deborah and Judith were daughters of the builder, Sam Hochman. One street in the development was named "Hochman Boulevard" until the homeowners rose in protest and renamed the street "Shelter Hill Road.")

My Aunt Anna had moved up to the Catskills to work in the hotels. My grandmother had died, so my grandfather moved with us to our new house, having his own room in what other suburban families called "the den." I remember my grandfather in his long blue overcoat, taking walks, looking like some old-world Tevye lost in the maze of suburban streets. He used to meet me at junior high to carry my books home. "*Luz mir truggin,*" he commanded in Yiddish. "Give it here!"

I begged my mother, "Couldn't you keep Papa home?" Apparently, she could not. I walked home from junior high with my friends, followed by a gaunt, eighty-year-old Jewish man carrying a pink loose-leaf notebook.

I went to college in the mid-sixties and majored in English education because I liked to read books, and my mother told me that if I became a teacher, I could still be home early enough to make dinner for my husband. Of course I went to college. Every Jewish high-school student I knew went to college. We never thought that *not* going to college was an option. While my grandparents had no formal schooling at all (my grandfather had taught himself to read both Yiddish and English) and most of my friends' parents had only high-school educations, my generation was simply expected to go to college.

My husband and I were in college at the same time: he attending a city university in Ohio; me, a state school in New York. His family—a mother and father both of whom could barely read English and who had not more than three years of formal education between them—also expected that their child would go to college, would make something of himself. Why else all those years of standing behind a cash register for fourteen hours a day in a grocery store? When my husband's book of short stories was published, he sent a copy to his mother; although she was unable to read it, she was proud to see his picture on the back.

The sixties were an exciting time to go to college. (Our own teenagers like to hear those stories now.) Talking about it together, Joe and I realize that we both had the same reaction to the sixties. That is, we didn't exactly fit. While we both sang folk songs, smoked some dope, and thought the war in Viet Nam was wrong, we also both couldn't buy into the flower-power, protest mentality that characterized that era. (Of course we didn't know each other at the time. This is some twenty years later we're sharing these revelations. We say: "Oh, you thought that? I thought that, too," amazed that we would have been sixties soul mates.) We thought we were hip then. We wrote poetry and grew our hair long. But part of it was the "America" thing, the way so many of our contemporaries saw America as the total bad guy and believed everyone poor and proletarian and third world was righteous and good.

I couldn't buy it. Living with a grandfather who used to bless the American dirt under his feet everyday—how could I sew an American flag onto the seat of my jeans? For Joe, the feelings ran even deeper. How could he demean a country that his family had risked its life to come to?

In college my husband and I were both English majors. That meant that we both read what was understood as the canon at the time: Hemingway, Fitzgerald, T. S. Eliot, Faulkner, Virginia Woolf. We both wrote term papers on *Death of a Salesman*. We both memorized Shakespearean sonnets. My husband wrote a short story about his passage from Lebanon, about how his older sister had typhoid fever and how his father had had to pinch her cheeks to give them color so no one would know the family had a sick child before they boarded the ship for America. I wrote a short story about my grandfather's leaving Russia. The first line was, "After all, he had seen the Czar . . ."

My husband and I followed that writer's adage: we wrote what we knew. And we followed the prescribed English major's curriculum: we read what they told us to. And all those years that we were writing and reading the same kinds of things helped to create the backdrop of aesthetic experience and historical reference that we share today.

We are, my husband and I, Arab and Jew, both Semites: same peoples, different tribes. Did I just say "tribes"? Maybe that's it. The reason for the long-held hatreds and animosity. The Lebanese have a saying: "My cousin and me against the world. My brother and me against my cousin." The intensity of the conflict comes from the shared rather than the dissimilar background.

There's a married couple who just moved to Ames and opened up a bakery. Refugees, lucky enough to flee from what was once Yugoslavia. He's a Croat and she's a Serb. Or perhaps she's a Croat and he's a Serb, I don't really know. That's part of the point, isn't it? Same peoples, different tribes. In Ireland: Protestant and Catholic; in Rwanda: Hutus and Tutsis. More alike than they are different. Don't they have trouble distinguishing who they are supposed to kill?

Tribal differences. Just a while ago, Joe and I were watching Arafat and Rabin on television, shaking hands after negotiating a peace treaty. How we long for peace in the Middle East: both for the survival of Israel and for the just treatment of the Palestinian peoples. What a great moment it was. Yet, watching Arafat, I was thinking: "Can we really trust them?" That is, can *we*, the Jews, trust *them*, the Arabs. I thought this sitting next to the man I trust the most in the whole world, who is more like me than any of the good friends I have made here in Iowa.

I can't even begin to sort out the divisions of power and the problems of economic disparity that continue to fuel the world's tribal conflicts. But I can reflect upon my own life and this kind-hearted and funny and passionate man whom I am fortunate enough to have as my husband. Is mine a cross-cultural marriage? I don't really think it is. Cross-cultural would be me marrying a Norwegian. An Iowa farmer. A Southern Baptist. Someone whose ancestors came over on the Mayflower. Someone with a gun in the back of the pickup. Someone who doesn't think that *Annie Hall* is a great movie. Someone without a highly developed sense of irony.

Other people might see this relationship as an irony in itself—the marriage between an Arab and a Jew—but my husband and I are more alike than different, our shared sensibility of the world cultivated by our love of literature, the immigrant narratives we grew up with, and the emotional tenor of the families we lived in. Arab and Jew, our cultures are not cleanly crossed but meshed into a complicated and rich mosaic where we are pleased to discover ourselves anew in this happy marriage of our middle age.

Enduring

A
PATCHWORK
LIFE

Catherine Casale

he roots of my story lie in a dislocated childhood, but the story I want to tell opens on a raw day in January 1982 when I boarded a plane and left America one month shy of twenty-three. On the eve of my departure, I told a friend that I felt as if I was giving birth to myself. I had been waiting many years to make this journey.

I flew from Boston to Tokyo via Toronto and Vancouver. In Vancouver the other Caucasians disembarked. My companions in the transit lounge were all Asians. With a change of planes I had become a minority and embarked on the exotic life I had been seeking. Three days later, I walked into my new job in a Japanese company and was served a cup of bitter green tea. The female staff who served the tea and then retreated were dressed in uniforms bearing the company logo. Male staff, dressed in their own clothes, pushed in close and asked when I planned to return to America to get married. With this question I realized that embracing the exotic encompassed more than I had reckoned on.

It is now 1995 and the bare biographical details read like this. I am a thirty-six-year-old American woman, married to an Englishman, raising a six year old and a three year old in Tokyo. Stated in black and white that sounds straightforward enough, but the truth is that for many years I've been riddled with doubts about who I am, what I am, where I want to live, and whether these questions even matter.

In the thirteen years I've lived overseas, my ideas about nationality and identity have been challenged repeatedly. I, in turn, have agonized continually over the questions of adaptation and assimilation. Much of the time I have floundered, feeling no more settled than a piece of flotsam tossed by the waves: I no longer feel entirely American, but I am not English, and not Japanese. An identity is more than a collection of negatives.

After considerable mental wrestling (more about that later), I've decided that nationality as part of one's identity does matter, and I'm determined to settle my residual uncertainties, not only for my sake, but for my children's. Yet if I no longer think of myself merely as an American, there is no reason my children ever should. My goal, therefore, is to create a balanced identity from the many strands of our lives. Ideally, this new identity will carry more emotional resonance than the term "global citizen." Perhaps for those of us who choose to complicate matters by living and marrying outside our native land, the birth of an intercultural identity is not a finite proposition.

One August morning when I had been working at my Japanese company for six months, I broke my teacup. Green tea is one of the social lubricants of Japanese life, and like all things Japanese, is bound in form and custom. At most daytime gatherings freshly prepared green tea is served in cups unmarred by handles. In offices, young female staff customarily serve green tea to the entire staff at ten and three o'clock along with a soy-seasoned rice cracker.

When I arrived in the winter, I had been given a cup left by a former employee. At the same time, it was suggested by my male colleagues that I join the tea-serving rota. Fresh from America with warnings about Japanese sexism jangling in my head, my plan was not to proselytize on the subject of equal rights — this was a foreign culture after all — but to opt for the male role whenever possible. In this case I made it clear that I did not consider serving tea an appropriate task for a rewriter.

But having refused my biological duty, I still felt uncomfortable accepting tea from my female colleagues, especially the company's first three women college graduates, who arrived with the April intake of new employees. Whether the Japanese women viewed me as a traitor to my sex, a deviant form of my sex, or a genderless, poorly socialized, and uncooperative foreigner, I do not know, but I made a point of serving my own tea from the instant tea machine. My hand-me-down cup was no more than an oversized thimble, and I vaguely intended to replace it with a "normal" sized cup or mug in order to save myself twenty trips a day to the tea machine.

On the morning I dropped my cup, a flurry of young women converged at my feet and whisked away the porcelain shards and spattered tea, while I, feeling yet again the clumsy *gaijin* ("foreigner"; literally, "outside person"), spluttered apologies. Sato-san, a leaden woman my age, who slaved as the office gofer in the quixotic hope of earning real responsibility, offered to take me to a pottery shop during our lunch hour. Looking after my assorted needs was one of Sato-san's appointed tasks.

After our usual lightning lunch in the company cafeteria, Sato-san led me across sweltering thoroughfares to a quiet back street of two-story shops-cum-dwellings hunkered one against the other. I pushed aside the sliding wooden door and squeezed into a narrow aisle between a table stacked high with plates and bowls, and floor to ceiling shelves crammed with sake sets, teapots, and cups.

Naturally, I gravitated toward the larger cups, cups capacious enough to handle an Earl Grey tea bag for those moments when a taste of home would be welcome. But every time I turned a cup in my hand, appraising its weight and texture and casting an eye over its design, Sato-san frowned and sucked in her breath. No good, no good, she murmured in Japanese, her severely cropped head trembling with restrained shakes. At first I was perplexed because I could see nothing aesthetically or functionally objectionable in the cups I was choosing. My reaction turned to exasperation as Sato-san's pursed lips and frown set into a rigid mask. Whose cup was this anyway?

Then it dawned on me that Sato-san, a living monument to the Japanese penchant for rules and regulations, was unlikely to be expressing her personal whims alone. Why? I asked. Sato-san blinked deeply several times. Why? Her puckered lips showed no signs of giving tongue. *Why?* Sato-san sighed heavily, then explained that the cups I was choosing were men's cups. I was expected to drink from a smaller, woman's cup.

I must have shown my astonishment in large, easy-to-read Western style because the hovering middle-aged proprietress now interceded. Ignoring me, she spoke in a persuasive manner to Sato-san, repeatedly mentioning that I was a foreigner. The finer points of the discussion were beyond my linguistic abilities, but I gathered that the proprietress was arguing that, as a foreigner, I could be exempted from the rules and use a man's cup. Sato-san was a forceful character (a woman of less resolve would not have endured the exploitation and petty humiliations she was subjected to daily in pursuit of a larger goal), and I could see that although the conversation was unusually animated, she wasn't budging. If I wished to maintain any semblance of culturally appropriate behavior, the answer was clearly no man's cup for me.

At this point, for me at least, it became a game. I held up a cup and the proprietress and Sato-san pronounced: man's or woman's. Finally, I found a cup that was ambiguous enough in size that neither woman could decide to which sex it belonged.

Sato-san remained unconvinced and muttered querulously as I handed over the cash, but I was thrilled, indifferent at this point to the cup's aesthetically unremarkable features. What this cup offered me was unaggressive size.

Only a week before I broke my teacup in Tokyo, I had been traveling in Korea. In every ceramics shop I had walked into, I'd come across what looked like pairs of mismatched teacups. American culture emphasizes the practical over the symbolic, and I assumed that the difference in size had something to do with function. I was wrong. A shopkeeper explained that the larger cup was for the man, and the smaller cup for the woman, as befitted their relationship and stations in life. When I recovered from my surprise, I bought a set as concrete proof of northeast Asia's sexism. I was only vaguely aware that the same custom prevailed in Japan. It never occurred to me that this custom, which might more accurately be called a rule, applied to me. That was their culture; I had my own.

I left the Japanese pottery shop elated, feeling that in skirting the omnipresent rules I had triumphed on some level. My first conscious culture shock soon set in. I had stumbled into the difference between a tourist who buys an ironic souvenir and a resident who is expected to buy the same offensive symbol for everyday use.

Until the teacup episode, I had spent six months finding most Japanese values and behavior patterns inimical to my American sensibilities. I was contemptuous of the mindless Japanese group-think I ran into everywhere I turned, horrified by a society that sacrificed 120 million individuals in the name of the common good. But the greater my disgust, the greater was my discomfort. For while my antipathy may have stemmed from American values, equally, as an American I felt that I had been educated to tolerate differences. Bouncing between a sense of personal failure and defensiveness, I debated whether my feelings were a legitimate reaction to what I was experiencing. I worried endlessly that my aversion to Japanese culture was no more than ethnocentric prejudice. I was further pierced by the dilemma of my antipathy's being at odds with my admiration for some of the results of Japanese social control. For example, in Tokyo, for the first time in my life, I experienced the complete absence of fear for my physical safety — an individual freedom I had never experienced in America. In short, I was wracked with confusion and anxiety, but none of that struck me as culture shock.

Now, suddenly, I realized that for six months I had been living under the false assumption that as a foreign woman I could pick and choose which social norms I wished to adhere to. I had been told ad nauseam by long-time foreign residents (mostly men in 1982) that as a *gaijin* I could "get away with anything." This statement always made me bridle. What did I need to get away with? I wanted to be accepted. I was willing to be culturally sensitive and play by the rules. Except, as I discovered again and again, I wasn't. And now I saw that in reality, as a woman, *gaijin* or not, I was expected to conform to Japanese standards much more closely than I had been led to believe.

I had moved out of the distantly located company dormitory into my own apartment after six weeks because the myriad rules of the women's dorm included a strict ten o'clock curfew. I resisted speaking in a teeny, tiny, tinsel voice as custom demanded of Japanese women. At casual lunches with colleagues I ordered what I wanted rather than following, lemminglike, the lead of the most senior member of the group.

In many ways I did conform. While I did not laugh or speak behind a cupped hand for modesty's sake, I did learn to harness my enthusiasm and speak in a quieter voice. I wore skirts and pantyhose even on weekends. In the privacy of my own home, I adhered strictly to the sacred rules regarding *tatami* mats (e.g., slippers are not allowed on *tatami* mats although vacuum cleaners are). I tried so hard not to be the ugly American abroad that I ended up feeling crushed.

Japanese society is structured to crush the individual (one popular Japanese proverb goes: The nail that sticks out will be hammered down), but I can't lay the blame for the intensity of my discomfort solely on Japanese society. I was suffering from a divisive internal struggle between a habitual desire to be invisible through superficial conformity, and a new set of social dictates that I found injurious to my soul. To complicate matters further, I was confronting a new reality: try as I might, invisibility was simply impossible for a foreigner to achieve in Japan. "*Gaijin. Gaijin,*" preceded and trailed my every step, from renting an apartment to walking down the street.

I spent the more than three years that I lived in Japan inwardly resenting and resisting the rules while outwardly conforming when I found it possible. In some areas I blatantly refused to conform but felt ill at ease. What's more, I lived with the disheartening suspicion that the efforts I did make were all for naught. I made adaptations the Japanese around me probably didn't even notice because the much grosser differences between us outweighed my stabs at Japaneseness. My former colleagues would probably express astonishment to hear that I made any adaptations at all.

Increasingly, the office had come to feel like a battleground of wills. It did not help that a bear market had set in and tensions were mounting in a business that depended on share turnover for revenue. No one had enough to do, which goes some way in explaining things. Another explanation is that my mere presence as a young woman who had traveled independently to a foreign country to work challenged every assumption these men held about life. Many of the men in the department needled me with a viciousness I still find shocking to recall. My superiors refused to give me any responsibility (or respect). The longer this situation persisted, and the more frustrated I became, the more stubbornly I refused to comply with their expectations of womanly behavior.

In my view, their sexist attitudes were where the problem lay. Sato-san's game plan was not for me. As far I as I could see, she wasn't getting anywhere with her bowing and scraping, and neither were the circumspect women graduates who kept their heads down and spoke when spoken to. Of course I was aware that my own "deviant" conduct could be contributing to the problem. But the cost to my self-esteem of adopting behavior that labeled me an inferior struck me as too dear.

In time, on the strength of that hated job and the freelance work I pursued with a vengeance, I landed a job as the representative for an American academic publisher. Overnight I left a climate of disapproval and rancor and assumed a position of responsibility. Japan's leading academics proved more imaginative than the analyst-salesmen in the international department of a second-tier securities company and simply dealt with my inconvenient sex by treating me as a de facto man. Over the next two years I enjoyed the most stimulating experiences of my working career. Sato-san turned twenty-five and retired from the company, as custom required, to marry a fishmonger.

I learned from my experiences in the securities company that even in a country like Japan, where foreigners are insistently pushed away and reminded that they cannot fit, on deeper levels they are expected to conform to the rules. In all societies there are fundamental beliefs that operate on a subconscious level as universal truths, not culturally bound customs. For the Japanese, small teacups for women are not a custom: they are a truth.

When you bump into other people's belief systems, you face behavioral decisions that run deeper than "When in Rome, do as the Romans do." For example, I was inwardly aggrieved by the rounded edges on my business card (women shouldn't have sharp corners), but as this was the social norm, I accepted it. In other words, I adapted. I started to get edgy about adaptation when the social norms extended to my personal teacup, which I did not see as an element of my job performance or professional persona, but which did impinge on my sense of self. When I was asked to serve tea, which clearly cast me in a subordinate role of prescribed limitations, I refused to adapt.

By the time I left Japan, I had made my peace with many of our differences. This was largely because of the luxury my job as the representative of a foreign firm afforded me. I was able to work in Japanese society while maintaining an official distance.

In my role as representative, I mediated between Japanese academics and Western colleagues who rarely understood each other's priorities. According to my colleagues in New York and London, I adhered to Japanese business etiquette to the extent that I was losing my Western perspective. I remained acutely conscious of just how many rules we were collectively breaking. When I listened to bitter complaints at face-to-face meetings over a cup of green tea or over intercontinental phone lines, I realized how far I had come. I had achieved a professional and personal balance where the two world views could mutually coexist. I was able to make this peace because I lived as an unintegrated outsider who had made adaptations.

Adaptation is both a form of cultural politeness and a matter of survival. It is also a necessary first step in assimilation. In Japan, a foreigner has no real hope of assimilating, and I had no interest in trying. Although I didn't know exactly where I was from in America, I had no doubts that I was American. Driven by curiosity, my goal, only partially facetious, was to live everywhere in the world. Assimilation wasn't really part of my thinking. I hadn't reckoned on what would happen in England.

The first year I lived in England I rejoiced daily that I no longer lived in Japan. I felt free. Provided I didn't wear sneakers, I was indistinguishable from a native until I opened my mouth. After three years of being stared at, leered at, propositioned, groped, discussed, and even shunned, I found this anonymity a relief.

In England I rediscovered the fullness of life. I adored London's architecture, dramatic northern skies, panoply of restaurants, textured language, and lively cultural smorgasbord. I didn't experience the culture shock that embittered Americans had warned me to expect in England. Coming as I did from Japan, what I noticed were the shared values of western European culture. Our differences struck me as mere trifles in the global scheme of things.

One blustery day in late August, I found myself on Oxford Street, where I'd been doing some last-minute shopping before a business trip to Japan and the States. It was late afternoon, and, in a sky that extended as far as the sea, a tumble of gilded clouds stood aloof from exuberant swathes of purples, reds, and blues. All around me harried shoppers yammered in different languages. Arab women sequestered behind *burqa* gathered their black robes and piled into roomy London cabs, Filipina maids in tow. Gaggles of brightly clad Italian teenagers leapt daredevil onto moving double-decker buses. The pinched British sagged beneath their parcels in jostling queues. Americans, dressed sensibly in sneakers and comfortable clothing, walked. I felt exhilarated. I felt more at home in that moment than I had felt anywhere at any time in my life. Eureka!

Life, unfortunately, isn't that simple, and as the years passed I became ambivalent about my life in England as an American. If my memory is to be trusted, this feeling emerged after I became engaged to an Englishman. Suddenly, the stakes changed.

One December day I was an American working in London and planning to enter a master's degree program at the University of London. The next day I was engaged and officially tied to the country. Over the Christmas holidays my mother-in-law-to-be dropped her chummy ways and started freezing me out. My brother-in-law-to-be was gratuitously insulting. Even my eighty-year-old grandmother-to-be caught the spirit and made a few swipes. I was not happy about these developments. I felt anything but welcomed to the family and land I was adopting as my own.

I suspected my future in-laws' change of behavior was caused by premarital qualms aggravated by cultural prejudice. I reasoned that any family might develop and express misgivings when a girlfriend became a fiancée; it is an individual step with family implications. I also knew from daily experience that the English widely view Americans as an inferior, boorish lot with an unfortunate grasp of the language. I was reminded of this in conversational repartee and over jolly word games as Christmas Eve merged into Christmas day, which blurred into Boxing Day. The preparation, eating, and clearing up of meals was punctuated with helpful advice: "If you had been to public school, Catherine, you would know that in England we do such-in-such in such-and-such a way." I protested, "Gerard went to public school, and he doesn't do it that way." "I'll explain it to you sometime."

The evidence for cultural prejudice amassed. I spent the festive period struggling to keep warm and seething with anger, hurt, and frustration. Behind closed doors Gerard counseled me to give as good as I got. He rejected my pleas for a show of support, saying that it was pointless for him to defend me. In his view, I needed to show his relatives that I would not tolerate bullying. I'm as familiar as the next person with that argument. I don't have trouble putting it into practice when necessary. But in this case I had been operating on the assumption that these new relatives were friends, not foes.

I had also assumed that my future husband and I would share as partners any turbulence that resulted from our alliance. Maybe English ideas about partnership were different from American ones. Maybe it wasn't mere chance that the concept of survival of the fittest had sprung from the head of an Englishman.

I did not know what to do — or even think. I balked at the idea that my familial survival depended on adopting behavior that, from my cultural perspective, meant lowering myself to an inferior standard of behavior. My conviction that my future relatives were behaving abominably was undermined by Gerard's remonstrations for cultural tolerance. I reconsidered. Maybe they weren't being mean and nasty. Maybe they were just enjoying a bit of good, clean fun English-style and I was too culturally blinkered to realize it. But try as I might to convince myself that the antagonism I sensed was solely a product of my own cultural narrowness, I did not believe it.

By preference, I would have acknowledged our cultural differences directly, but getting the English to deal squarely with such a meaty issue is as difficult as getting them to admit to an American that England has class problems. In the end I adopted an English solution: I muddled through and made the best of a bad job. The holidays ended and I returned gratefully to our life in London.

In January Gerard's uncle gathered the clan for a roast meal. These occasions have a life cycle of their own. They hatch when the door is shut against the unmerciful climate and the guests glide into the cozy sitting room for appetizers. Two hours later, warmed but ravenous, friends and relations unwind before a table laden with fine wines, roast beef, roast potatoes, roast parsnips and carrots, buttered swede, and green beans. The guests dine, as boa constrictors devour, the prey that will sustain them for months. Bloated bellies ignored, the meal ends with vigor: fruit salad and mousse followed by bread and cheeses, coffee, liqueur-filled chocolates, and *digestifs*.

At this meal, in common with the ones before it, a good deal of merry American baiting was going on. As always, I was one American among many Brits. And on this occasion I was fed up. I decided that it was time to follow Gerard's advice and demonstrate my mettle.

The subject turned to America's pusillanimous behavior in the first and second world wars. The Americans were cowards. They came in too late. They acted out of self-interest. My knowledge of history was deeper than the others', and I argued hard against their judgments. I tried to balance their nationalistic, emotional views with a range of perspectives. But I made no headway. It became clear that this was not a rational debate—the kind of discussion the English can excel at—but a xenophobic orgy. It was also bullying.

On my left, Nigel, an old friend of Gerard's uncle, demanded to know where the Americans had been while the English had stoically endured the Blitz. Where had the Americans been when England needed them? What had America done for England? I felt the others watching me, waiting for my answer.

I faced Nigel and said, "If it weren't for the Americans, the English would be speaking with German accents." Nigel looked apoplectic. I flushed. I watched his twitching lips and listened to the silence. I felt seared by nine pairs of eyes. Silence. I told myself I'd drunk too much wine and Gerard would never forgive me. And what about his mother? Gerard's uncle cleared his throat, rubbed his hands together, and suggested dessert. I peeked at Gerard. His twinkling eyes met mine.

One damp, grey, gloomy, typically god-awful February day, Gerard and I scrabbled through a refuse-littered back alley in Soho. The skies threatened sleet. We were making our way home from the wholesale bakery, where moments before we had ordered a traditional English wedding cake. Fruitcake. Yuck. I can't bear the stuff. I looked around me and asked myself: Can I live in this country for the rest of my life?

Gerard was ahead of me, his head bent low against the wind. A nagging worry flew from my lips, "How are we going to run our finances after we get married?" I can't remember his answer, but I wasn't satisfied. I stopped in my tracks like a mule scared by a twig in the road. Gerard stopped too — exasperated — couldn't we talk about this once we were inside and warm? I didn't budge. Predictably, the conversation grew testy. We both got riled up. Surrounded by garbage and crumbling Victorian walls, the damp cold like acid in my bones, I worked myself into a state of abject uncertainty. The moment I half-consciously had been seeking had arrived; I toyed with the idea of breaking the engagement.

But I didn't. I loved my husband-to-be and I decided to trust in that love. I decided that the fear that had been poisoning my joy could not be resolved. I feared that I would end up like the deeply homesick middle-aged people I had met who lived wistfully in their spouses' native lands. Could I make a decision at the age of twenty-seven that meant giving up my country? When I had left the States five years before it had been for a sojourn — not for life. It was motivated by a desire to explore the rest of the world rather than a rejection of America.

In the end I decided that I couldn't predict whether I would even be alive in twenty years to be yearning for my home country. I decided not to throw away the present for fear of the future. I loved this man and wanted to be with him. We made up, went home, and no doubt drank a nice cup of tea (the English answer to every woe).

On the afternoon of our March wedding the wind gusted wildly. Raindrops splashed under a strong sun. Rainbow conditions. Members of the wedding party and our guests turned their faces to the sun as they stood waiting on the front steps of Chelsea's Old Town Hall. Our hired photographer sidled up to my brother-in-law and asked whether it was a marriage of convenience. Later at our reception we heard that lashing winds had sent stones from the Old Bailey clock tower tumbling into the streets below. In the land of Shakespeare I found myself wondering whether tumultuous winds were a portent.

In Japan I worked and lived in Japanese society but socialized mostly with Americans. In England I experienced total cultural immersion. I lived in England for three years before I made an American friend. By marrying an Englishman, I acquired an English family. Over time, and without even noticing it, my language and manner began to change. It was as if by marrying my husband in England, I was expected to make all the adaptations. It was a subtle process. Others subconsciously expected it of me, and I came to expect it of myself. This process came to take on the characteristics of assimilation. To my English friends and relatives my own country remained an unknown abstraction, or worse, an abstraction known only through fast-food franchises and Hollywood images.

At the time of our marriage, my husband had never even traveled to the States, so it is not as if he understood my country any better than his countrymen, but we did share another cultural bond. For three years we had lived within two minutes' walk in the same lower middle-class neighborhood in western Tokyo. Curiously, despite our proximity in a vast city where foreigners were in conspicuously short supply, neither of us pursued friendship. Our relationship was limited to the occasional nod as we passed on the street. Considering that we later found each other's company compelling enough to marry, our reserve is puzzling. I think it is partially explained by the cultural differences that polarize American and English relations, even in a place like Tokyo, where Westerners tend to feel linked by their common status as "outside people." Our national senses of humor, fun, and good conversation are often at odds.

When my husband and I met again in London, our national identities were in transition. We may have been English or American by birth, but this was superseded to some extent by the intensity of an early adulthood spent in the strange isolation that characterizes the life of *gaijin* in Japan. What's more, in London we found ourselves *gaijin* all over again. At the time I felt so marked by my time in Tokyo that I wondered whether I would ever feel meaningfully connected to people who hadn't lived in Japan. British and visiting American colleagues laughed at quirky habits, such as excessive gift giving or bowing when on the telephone or paying taxi drivers. My husband, who for five years had been repeatedly counseled by his Japanese company to be patient in keeping with the Japanese way, wondered whether he would ever catch up with his English peers in his career. We were surrounded by people whose only conception of Japan came from a popular television program's exposés of barbaric Japanese cultural practices. We seldom spoke together of Japan because there was no need to — we already understood. The starting point of our relationship was the comfort of this shared cultural background.

Yet when my relationship with Gerard shifted from the casual to the serious, any concerns I had about our differing nationalities were overshadowed by the fear that his particular constellation of skills would inevitably mean a return to Japan for another protracted stint. A few years later a change of jobs indeed brought with it a posting to Tokyo. I spent the year before we returned to Japan dreading it. When acquaintances asked how long we were going for, I joked that we'd been given a sentence of three to five years. Inside, I wasn't joking.

The last year we lived in London, I was tending to our one-year-old and making slow progress on a master's thesis. In the middle of making the beds or vacuuming, I would clutch up in fear: I could not face that endless city of concrete swarming with people again. I couldn't go. I couldn't stay. The States wasn't a viable option. By the time I finished ticking off my options, I lay in a heap on the floor weeping, while a few feet away my son investigated the rubber plant's soil. I felt utterly homeless.

In the early years of my international life, I had felt empowered by my easy familiarity with a number of cities across the globe. Now I was experiencing the dark side of that life. My misgivings about the future that I imagined in Tokyo spread like mold to the present in London. If I didn't want to live in Tokyo, what exactly was keeping me in London? As I opened the doors and drawers of my life in England, I saw thick green fur everywhere.

An accumulation of petty slights for an inferior accent, inferior education, inferior manners, and inferior culture—all seemingly small and transitory in themselves—had begun to weigh me down and sour me. It is not that my experiences in England changed significantly after marriage, but the depth of my reactions did. The stakes had changed for me too. What formerly could be ignored now mattered. This wasn't playing at living overseas. This was for keeps. With pregnancy had come a yearning to live in the States again. But by that time Americans mistook me for a Brit. Who was I? What was I? I felt bereft of a community of peers or a place I could call home.

With the birth of our son my responsibilities had changed, and my old desire to wander had waned. I did not want to pass on a legacy of rootlessness. Yet here we were, a once-upon-a-time American and an Englishman, setting off to raise our child in a third country. I realized that with the parenting challenges I faced, the time had come to resolve my increasingly tortured questions of nationality and identity. But how?

After a few of these downward-spiraling panic attacks, I decided that I preferred drama on the stage and took some practical steps. First, I arranged to audit a graduate course on Japanese economic history to broaden my relationship with Japan from the practical and emotional spheres to the intellectual. Then I started studying Japanese again. By the time my husband, son, and I boarded the plane for Tokyo, I had come to believe on an emotional level that I was entering a new life and not a rehash of the earlier one. But I was no closer to resolving my identity problems.

In the five-and-a-half years I had been away, Tokyo had changed and so had I. For one thing, I no longer bridled at the term *gaijin*. What had once been a burden now felt like a liberating persona. In England I felt as if I was expected to improve myself by adopting English customs and masking my true identity. In Japan I am a foreigner, pure, simple, and always. No matter what efforts I make to assimilate, there is no expectation on the part of the Japanese that I will fit on a meaningful level. So after five years in England as a damn Yank, I found relief in the impersonal anonymity of life as a generic *gaijin*. I finally understood the nature of the freedom those foreign men had promised me in 1982.

We have been living in Tokyo on an expatriate package for four years, and, after two uneven years of adjustment, I can say I enjoy this life despite its drawbacks. As an expat mother not working outside the home, I don't participate in Japanese society. I move through it as an observer on the most peripheral level. I plan my life around avoiding the train crush, the traffic jam, the movie mob, the restaurant rush, the museum queue, the plane reservation overload, and the three-dollar apple. But Tokyo life is a crushed life, so I live with the shoving crowds and packed trains, the typhoons and earthquakes, as part of dwelling on Japanese soil. I barely interact with any Japanese other than those whose jobs involve serving the public.

This has meant that I've learned little new about Japan, but a lot about myself. I think this is because the life of an expat in Asia is an odd one, disembodied from the local culture and from one's own. In London we lived an English life. Here we can "get away with anything." In Tokyo's amorphous international community I have made American friends and reconnected with my roots. Equally, I have slipped into a comfortable, if ill-defined, international identity. Weird? Maybe. I know our family needs to leave this strange, bubblelike existence sometime. We will benefit from being grounded in a society where we are all fluent in the language and are invested in and accountable to the society at large.

In the meantime, my life revolves around international school schedules, and before I know it the June migration is upon us, when women and children undertake twenty-four-hour journeys for two to three months of annual "home leave." We leave to escape the summer humidity, to find some green, and to give our children a sense of where they come from other than Japan. We see friends and relatives once a year as summer gypsies, entirely outside the context of our lives. With each passing year the distance grows. They have no idea how we live or have changed and exhibit a conspicuous lack of curiosity about our lives. By late August, after nine weeks living out of suitcases in other people's homes, I gratefully embrace the blanket of humidity that marks our return to Tokyo. I collapse in our front hall, surrounded by suitcases bursting with a year's worth of shopping and the distinctive smell of our apartment's carpeting, and I think, "I am home."

It isn't a turbulence-free landing. The expat community is highly transient, and each September I find myself mourning the loss of my friends and the children's friends while gearing up to make new ones. I do this while recovering from the emotional upheaval of the annual visit to former and potentially future homes. As expats we live with the specter of being recalled and forced, at two weeks' notice, to dismantle a family life painstakingly fashioned from pieces. When we moved to Tokyo, we came with the conscious goal of creating the first home our son would remember. In our last year in London, I decided that if circumstances hadn't given me a feeling of home, the answer was to create one myself. I took inspiration from the proverb, "Home is where the heart is." I was tired of living like a transient.

Yet by the time I return to Tokyo each August, I feel like a world-class transient. Good times and bad times in once and future homes have the effect of unraveling the delicate weave of my tenuously fabricated identity as an American-born-Global-Citizen-Married-to-an-Englishman. A September 1994 journal entry captures the mood: *Everything is all stirred up after the summer. I'm feeling crummy about all the old issues. I've debated them inside out and upside down a few dozen times in the past few weeks. I'm exhausted to death. I want a lobotomy. I want to take my overactive, insistent imagination to dog-training school and give it a good yank on the choke-collar when it even thinks of sniffing one of its favorite bushes (e.g., As an American can I ever be happy living in England long-term? Or, Am I even an American anymore? Or even better, Now that I'm so inextricably confused can I ever be happy or fit in anywhere or am I destined to bounce around this planet as an outsider until my dying days?).*

I know now to expect similar rocky patches and periods of doubt at transitional moments of my life. It is the nature of the life I am leading, but a temporary blip does not negate my newfound clarity of identity. I hope this identity is resilient enough to withstand the hostility I will experience again when we return to England. I say hope, because an identity is not an impermeable concept that travels intact. At least mine isn't. I want to stay open to the challenges that involvement with another culture brings, even if it means a little angst along the way.

When we first returned to Japan, my friend Corbin sent me a card with a photograph of an exuberant patchwork quilt. The text explained that a patchwork quilt is made from hundreds of pieces of cloth. Corbin's jaunty note said, "Does this remind you of your life?" Unfortunately, it did, and I filed the card away and have not been able to lay my hands on it since. I've looked for that card more than once over the years because with time I realized that I had missed the point. I was so busy feeling grim about my patchwork life that I wasn't allowing myself to embrace it.

From the time I was a child I have thrilled to the joyous, colorful designs of patchwork quilts, lovingly assembled from chaotic scraps and transformed into living art. When we bought a house in London, I saved the extra material from our first curtains and tucked them away in the attic. I harbor the dream of one day gathering together all the curtain remnants of all the houses and apartments and countries we have ever lived in and having them made into patchwork quilts. If I can celebrate the beauty of a patchwork quilt, I can celebrate the beauty of my own life.

DENMARK'S
A PRISON

Lita Page

Hamlet. Denmark's a prison.
Rosencrantz. Then is the world one.
Hamlet. A goodly one, in which there are many confines,
wards, and dungeons, Denmark being one o' th' worst.

HAMLET 2.2

t's a fairyland of low crime and a high standard of living. According to the statistics, it ranks among countries with the highest quality of life. But how do you measure quality of life? What some back office in the United Nations thinks of quality of life is not my version. It doesn't take into account the number of hours of daylight in the dead of winter or the total available shopping hours year round. The statisticians don't measure local hostility to foreigners or how insular a culture can be.

My husband, Keith, told me he would be paying sixty-five percent of his salary to the government for the privilege of living in his own country. As soon as I arrived in Copenhagen, I started making mental notes on what we would be provided with. We would get free medical care, subsidized dentistry, schools, and unlimited unemployment pay and welfare.

"You'll feel very safe there," he said before we arrived. "Safe," what a strange word to use. I suppose he meant secure. The security of knowing that if I should become unemployed, a single mother, or mentally unfit, I would be taken care of by the welfare state for life. The security of knowing that heinous crimes like serial killings and violent carjackings were nearly nonexistent. Sure I felt safe on the trains and buses. After a while I let my guard down, left my handbag wide open while I walked around town. I walked around in a daze like most of the Danes. Mothers leave their babes outside the bakery and post office, and they are still there when they come out. Street wisdom and alertness are not necessary in Denmark. The kind of radar one uses in New York City or any similarly violent Third World capital is not required here, at least not now. Even the queen of Denmark has been known to walk around by herself. A friend told me she met up with her alone in a department store elevator. If my friend had been a "Squeaky Frome" type, she could have iced Her Majesty right there.

As I tasted the security of Denmark, I also noticed how it breeds mediocrity. Except for the Danish ballet and the pastries, which are world-class, everything was second-rate. The books published were lousy, the local theater was a joke, the newspapers were run by amateurs, and the cafes served bad and ridiculously high-priced food. The sheer price of food was enough to send anyone running from the supermarket screaming, except for Swedes or Norwegians, who regularly shop Denmark for the "bargains." The television programs were horrible American rip-offs, with unprofessional production standards that made TV reporters look like ghouls in baggy clothes. The lack of consumer advocacy and the high taxes were allowing substandard products and high prices to dominate the marketplace.

Garrison Keillor thinks Denmark is charming, and I do not. In fact, shortly after I arrived, I began complaining to my husband about all his country's shortfalls. Since I had worked for a

Danish company outside Denmark, I had already been in the habit of Dane-bashing with my colleagues. But now my Dane-bashing had to be directed to Keith, my husband, and he took it personally. I think he continued to take it personally. This was surprising after the traveling and living abroad he had done. I had ceased years ago to be protective about Americans, their presidents, culture (or its supposed nonexistence), Vietnam, racism, tribal genocide, or CIA interference in the Third World. An American abroad in the last few decades usually gets blasted with one or more of these issues.

Keith and I fell in love and married in England, on neutral ground where neither of us had family or emotional ties. At first he felt self-conscious about his English, but we had a spiritual, emotional, and physical attraction that made up for it. We had both worked for the same company for years without knowing each other, and we had many mutual colleagues. His gentility and refined European flair were very attractive to me, and in turn he found me very exotic. "I feel like I am part of some Italian movie," Keith said, just after meeting me.

We moved to Denmark after being married for two years. I tried to learn Danish. But Danes would crane their necks to try to understand a slightly mispronounced word. They were not used to hearing their language in the mouths of foreigners. Unlike English speakers, whose dialects and accents worldwide can fill volumes, the Danes aren't used to having foreigners mispronounce words. So people would ask me to repeat myself or look at me blankly. Some friends would just laugh or giggle. Keith would shake his head in disgust or wait until after the party to tell me all the things I said wrong. I stopped speaking Danish in front of him until I got it right. It took three years.

We lost some degree of emotional intimacy. One theory I had was that I was Dane-bashing too much and too often. But he was preoccupied with work and was in the office most weekends. There was no joy anymore, no light-heartedness. He had left it behind in England. His work environment in Copenhagen was not as stimulating; it was full of dull routine after the international ambience of London. He often spoke of a new career in social work or teaching.

I continued soaking up local color. My Danish improved, and I was thoroughly versed in all the rituals. Upon entering someone's house for a meal, you would thank them profusely for inviting you. The host would then thank you profusely for bringing a gift of chocolates/flowers/plants. During the dinner you would raise your glasses for a *skøl* and make sure you looked into everyone's eyes before putting your drink down. With wineglass raised, the host would thank the guests again for the gifts. After the evening was over, you would thank them profusely for having you and for the victuals. Your host would then say farewell (literally, *farvel*) and bid you a safe journey home. I used to imagine how thousands of Danes were uttering the same words at the same moment all around Denmark.

As each season passed, I would learn all the special songs associated with holidays and birthdays. This was so that I would not look out of place at family gatherings and could blend in. I even began writing songs in Danish for these occasions, like many Danes, but I felt unappreciated. This was an enormous personality change for me and against my principles of individualism. Here I was conforming to a culture that seemed to value mediocrity. I just wanted to blend in because it felt "safe." Almost the only time I didn't try to conform was on the beach, when young and old, saggy and thin, stripped their clothes off as soon as the temperature went above sixty-five degrees. I drew the line there.

I knew something was wrong when I began to hate the sound of bicycles at rush hour. To me, it symbolized the Danes' lack of personal income instead of a healthy energetic method of transportation. Just watching a cyclist pedaling along the designated lanes in pouring rain would depress me. Why isn't this person in a nice, warm, dry car?

I told Keith to start thinking about leaving Denmark permanently or at least temporarily. My sanity and well-being were at stake. He didn't dismiss my feelings but took this news in his usual quiet and understated Scandinavian manner.

Just as I began to plan my escape from Denmark, Keith became seriously ill while on a business trip. Instead of consulting a doctor while traveling, my stubborn husband just took aspirin for a week to alleviate a high fever. I had to rush him from the airport to a hospital in Copenhagen.

Keith was suffering from a serious case of pneumonia, and after some tests the doctors drew some pretty sinister conclusions. Here was a conservative Scandinavian bank executive being told he had full-blown AIDS. I felt like the guillotine was now hovering above our heads. Keith just sobbed most of the first weekend, all the while hooked up to a respirator. He nearly didn't make it through that weekend, and once the diagnosis sank in, he screamed, "I'm not one of them!" referring to the high-profile drug addicts and homosexual victims of AIDS. This reaction shocked me because I believed him to be more compassionate than that. But Keith was always into appearances, liked to flaunt his new suits and yuppie lifestyle. Besides being terribly weak and unable to breathe properly, he felt like he was being lumped in with "them."

Once they stabilized Keith, the doctors and nurses immediately got on my case and started insisting I was in danger along with my eighteen-month-old son. One nurse even took my arm and tried to escort me out of Keith's room and down the hall for an HIV test. I jerked back from the nurse, said no thank you, and went to find my son, who was in another patient's room. I found him chatting, in toddler gibberish, to an elderly lady who, it turned out, was dead. As I pulled him from the room, the hospital morgue cart arrived.

It was a ghoulish environment, and it felt like living through a nightmare in which I had to escape being labeled "AIDS family of the week." It was just the sort of front-page tabloid drama I wanted to avoid. Not only did I ignore all this talk about HIV tests because my son and I were perfectly healthy, I agreed with

Keith that few people should be told. The implications and reactions were too horrendous to contemplate.

Once I pulled myself from the chasm of shock, I started to
make calls to the States to find information about treatments,
drugs, and tests. The more I discovered, the less I listened to the
Danish doctors. They continued pleading with me about getting tested. "You'll know once and for all," said one doctor.
"You'll stop thinking about it," said a nurse. They sat with their
arms across their chests as if being assaulted when I proclaimed,
"Frankly, I think about my own condition less and less each day
and become stronger about fighting for my husband's survival."
They didn't dig it, this foreign broad challenging their opinions.

Their answers to my fundamental questions were conflicting.
Every time I asked about the statistics concerning children of
HIV-positive or AIDS parents, it would be a different number.
One nurse said 29% and another said 50%. One doctor said
12% and another said 19%. This was unacceptable. After what I
had witnessed in that hospital, I would never let these medical
robots near me or my son. I would never put myself in their
hands.

Besides having no confidence in their knowledge, I could
only deal with Keith's illness. I could not help him if I and/or
my son were labeled potential AIDS cases by these charlatans,
and Keith could only deal with Keith. The very mention that
my son or I could be infected by HIV would send Keith over
the edge. He would sob as I had never seen him sob before. It
was detrimental to his health to dwell on the unthinkable.

During those early days in the hospital, I fed him vitamins on
the sly, brought him home-cooked meals twice a day, bathed
him, and took him to the bathroom. I made notes about the
medication he was taking and the tests he was undergoing. The
head doctor complained to Keith that I was asking too many
questions. When Keith complained about heavy side effects
from his drug therapy, the doctor on duty that day looked
mystified and acted as if she had never heard of side effects be-

fore. I was now incredibly uncomfortable about the care he was receiving.

We told few people, only the immediate families, about the diagnosis. I never even asked Keith where he thought he contracted the virus, and he never volunteered any theory. I believed it was pointless to waste emotional energy on the subject when facing such a major health crisis — though our families would continue to harp on this theme throughout and ask inappropriate questions about the origin of the illness.

It took Keith's family a long time to accept that he was seriously ill with AIDS. It didn't make any sense to them. One brother just knocked his head repeatedly against the hospital's stone walls in shock when I told him. Keith was so traumatized by the social stigma that he refused to join individual or group therapy. His brother went in his place and attended weekly meetings in the AIDS/HIV crisis center. As Keith developed new AIDS-related illnesses, his family began treating him as if he were a walking corpse. Their negativity had a profound effect on Keith, as did the assembly-line medical treatment.

I concentrated my efforts on researching all the new holistic modalities being tried in the United States by a large number of AIDS survivors. Attitude seemed the key to long-term survival. On the surface, Keith seemed to have the fighting spirit and wanted to regain quality of life. But there was too much Dane in him, not enough independent spirit to question the doctors and the treatments. He never quarreled with them even if they misdiagnosed him, mistreated him, ignored him, or gave him conflicting information.

After the first illness, he was gaining weight and doing well. We were supplementing his local medical care by phoning doctors in New York City, who would advise on nutrition, exercise, and vitamin/mineral treatments. Keith had left his bank job and was on a generous pension. Though all his custom-made suits hung unused in the closet, he didn't seem to mind abruptly leaving his job. He assured me that he never missed it.

At first I was a saint in his eyes. Keith would get teary and emotional when talking about what I must have been going through and how I was taking care of him. Later I found an entry in his diary, written in Danish, "My wife's love and support warms me deep in my soul." It was the kind of language and emotion he had never verbalized. We had eventually reached, after seven years of marriage, a kind of bicultural communication. Our sentences were half English and half Danish, and we had certain pat phrases in both languages we would use only in private.

Everything was going well, and we planned to spend the winter away from Denmark, when he developed a second infection that was misdiagnosed and left untreated for six weeks. This debilitated him again, and the drugs weakened him physically and mentally. Though he had to take an IV treatment daily, he faced it with great courage and tenacity. He knew exactly how to mix the drugs, prepare the equipment, and administer himself. I would do anything for him except handle needles or inject. I never would make a good drug addict.

The misdiagnosis of two serious conditions threatened his sight and his life. It was a combination of Keith, his own brother and sister (both doctors), and the hospital staff that bungled the diagnosis. My frustration was now intense, and I was without much energy to voice it. I felt that Keith was risking his life by having faith in the Danish medical system and listening to his siblings, who knew less about HIV and AIDS than I finally did.

The complacency of the Danes and complete acceptance of authority was at the root of this medical crisis. I came from a culture where authority, even the medical profession, was open for challenge. Everything is negotiable in life, in my opinion, but no one in Denmark seemed to agree with me.

It was frustrating knowing that no one around Keith besides me felt the system inadequate. The only time Keith didn't go along with the system was when they tried to sign him up as a guinea pig in a triple-blind test of AZT, DDI, and another drug. Keith told me that of the eight doctors he saw during a one-week hospital stay, four of them whispered to him that they would never take AZT, and four said that he'd better start taking AZT. Keith had no control over who his doctors were or what kind of treatment he was offered. Of course it was all free — tests, visits, and drugs — but it was at the expense of knowing a specific doctor or getting complete information about the drugs. I only attended a few of Keith's regular checkups. During the long waits for testing and consultation, the drug addicts would make themselves known by quarreling with the staff and each other. Keith was visibly shaken by these episodes. I had seen so many similar scenes while living in New York that it didn't shock me.

Once we finally saw a doctor, Keith would feel uncomfortable if I asked too many questions. He would volunteer little information to the doctor, and the doctor wouldn't press him. We later would joke about these consultations when Keith was seriously emaciated. I asked him what the doctor said, and Keith sarcastically imitated the doctor ("Everything fine, good, see you next month"), who didn't bother mentioning or even noticing that Keith, a six-footer, weighed ninety pounds and looked like a concentration camp victim.

I stopped attending his consultations and would remain in the waiting room with the hostile drug addicts. Keith didn't mind going in alone, and if I didn't attend, he could avoid the questions about my HIV status that would be raised at every visit.

Our whole lifestyle revolved around the illness. After six months, I had to preserve what little energy I had left. I could only take care of Keith away from Denmark, preferably some place warm, if only temporarily. I felt as if I was on some remote planet called Denmark and had to find my way home by clicking my heels like Dorothy. Keith's family were aliens in my book, and their fatalistic approach was killing him and me both.

They were shocked and outraged that we would leave Denmark and the wonderful care Keith was receiving. They were concerned that we couldn't get emergency care, but they were really fearful that he would die abroad, away from them.

We did travel for awhile, but Keith returned to Denmark frequently for checkups and treatment. Each time he was a little weaker, and each time he went abroad, he would gain weight and get stronger. By the time he agreed to go full time under a doctor's care in New York, it was too late. His mental attitude had changed. He was weak and going blind. The Danish doctors refused him further treatment, though I located a doctor in Texas who was willing to treat him for free and possibly restore partial sight in one eye. It was the last set of phone calls I made trying to second-guess the Danish doctors. No one would listen to me in Denmark or help me get Keith and his medical records to Texas. Keith and his family accepted the Danish hospital's conclusion that precious treatment shouldn't be wasted on someone in his condition. The fact that they sacrificed his sight and health without even a fight broke me. The frustration was going to eat me alive if I continued on that course. I stopped pestering Keith about fighting the health battle and just served his basic needs.

After eighteen months, I could see a profound change in his condition and mental state. One evening I said softly to him, "We've been through bad times before and you pulled through, but if you want to let go, it's OK with me, just let go." He died at my side ten minutes later. It was a calm and peaceful death. I am very grateful it could happen at home, away from what would have been a hospital circus.

Though I could now leave Denmark for good, I carry an eternal scar from the narrow-mindedness that helped hasten my husband's death, rendering me an emotionally overwrought widow and my son fatherless at the age of three. The gates were opened, but I walked out of the prison called Denmark with a heavy heart.

UNDERCURRENTS

JoAnn Hansen Rasch

 "Sign here please," said the clerk, pushing the marriage contract across the table. I picked up the fountain pen and started to write. Then I stopped.

"Which name?" I asked.

A murmur of sounds, English, French, and Swiss German, swirled about the room. My new patent-leather handbag slipped to the floor as I curled my legs under the chair. I looked up and saw my future husband smiling, his eyes filled with love and a bit of condescension, which I had already decided belonged to every man I'd met. But there was something else that I didn't want to see.

"Darling, put our name of course."

I smiled back gratefully. Peter would always be there to help me. He was like a solid rock in the agitated rapids of my life. But it was only after I had written down his name, placing it awkwardly next to mine, that I admitted to his swaggering glow of possession.

Peter continued to beam at me while our witnesses signed the paper. I knew that I should be like that, too, but I just wanted to get through the day without creating an international faux pas.

The clerk stood up and we all followed.

"I wish you happiness," he said, as he briefly touched my fingers.

"*Merci beaucoup,*" I replied. It was frustrating to speak so little French. Suddenly, my mind seemed choked by swamp weed.

Emma, who as my witness had been sitting next to me, turned and hugged me.

"Well dear, what's it like to be a married woman?" she asked in her limpid British accent.

"I don't feel anything," I answered truthfully.

She laughed, hugged me again, and then kissed Peter. She appeared much older than I remembered, with her dark hair piled into a beehive and her face carefully made up. I could hardly recognize my friend from boarding school.

My father-in-law pulled me to his chest. He was pleased with me. During the last weeks since that difficult Sunday when Peter had announced to his parents that I was pregnant, we had learned to appreciate one another. He believed that my union to his son was ineluctable even though I was only eighteen years old, professionally unqualified, and a foreigner. I was, nevertheless, the sort of girl you married.

As he kissed me on each cheek, I remembered the evening, a few days ago, when he had returned from work and had called us into the living room. He stood in the center of the room with his hands behind his back.

"I've got a present for you both," he said. "Dianne, you choose first." I pointed to the left and he brought round his arm, revealing an antique Irish decanter. He handed it to me and another one to Peter.

"Oh, they're lovely," I said, touched by the unexpected gesture. The bottles represented all the personal possessions that belonged in a home. I hadn't even dared to think about it, but now, as I traced a finger over the translucent crystal, I could imagine my own place.

"What a ridiculous idea," his wife stated. She wiped her hands on the tea towel that she had carried in from the kitchen. "A useless present. What they need are some dishes or some baby clothes."

"No," I said, balancing the decanter carefully as I tried to hold on to Peter's father. "They're exactly right." But he had only shrugged his shoulders and turned away to his desk, where he laid out a game of solitaire while he waited for his wife to serve dinner.

Now, receiving my father-in-law's congratulations, I remembered how the decanters looked on the coffee table in the new apartment. It seemed hard to believe those graceless little rooms would be home that night. I pulled away from my father-in-law. My cheeks burned, and once again I plunged into anxiety. I didn't know anything about housekeeping or cooking, let alone caring for a baby. A few weeks ago, I had still been living at boarding school.

Across the rows of chairs Daddy was observing me. He lifted one hand as if to wave at me. It seemed both an encouragement and a warning. I could see that he was on his best behavior, and he wanted me to be the same. I nodded my head to reassure him. It was all right. I was legally married to the man I loved, his family welcomed me, and I would never be lonely again.

I turned to my husband. His lips against mine were dry and resolute.

"Now you're Swiss. Tomorrow we'll get your passport."

Surprised, I stared at him. Up until that moment I had never considered changing nationalities. I had married a man, not a nation. My New Zealand passport was enough. I was proud to be a Kiwi from Down Under. Hadn't I spent the last seven years, after my family immigrated to the United States, refusing to become an American citizen? But Peter looked so content. I knew what it meant for him to offer me his nationality. So many people wanted to have the red passport with the white cross, and I couldn't be ungracious and tell him it wasn't necessary. An idea came to me.

"Thank you, darling. In exchange, I'd like to take out papers for you to become a New Zealander." Peter's eyes widened.

"I don't want to. I'm Swiss," he announced. The clerk coughed, closed his register, and moved toward the door. Our time was up. Peter put his arm around my waist.

"Come on," he said. Clutching me against him, he crushed our discussion with the strength of his will. We would not talk about it again. He lead me out of the room.

In the square, housewives were doing their daily shopping. It was market day in Vevey, and portable stands, displaying carrots and leeks, were lined up around the edge of the streets. The sun felt warm — so far the winter had been mild — and the lake lay calmly mirroring the snowy mountains. We all stood on the stone steps against the heavy wood doors, while Daddy adjusted his camera. I turned and kissed Peter.

"That's a great picture," Daddy said.

"I want to take some, too," Emma said, leaving her position on the steps, as she looked for her camera in her handbag. I waited patiently, smiling at everyone. We all smiled.

Afterwards, we drove up to my parents-in-law's house, which was situated above the old town. They were Swiss German, but they had lived in the French part of Switzerland for many years. Peter was their only child.

My mother-in-law had spent our wedding morning preparing the lunch. In the dining room an embroidered cloth was spread over the table. Two women in starched linen aprons had come to help. They showed us where to sit.

"Dianne," my father-in-law said, "I've found a very special Bordeaux. It was made the year you were born." He carefully offered the bottle to me. My father-in-law was initiating me into the luxuries of the old continent.

Peter poured me a glass. When everyone was served, we were toasted and once again wished a lifetime of happiness. The wine tasted of moist humus. I let it settle inside me. It made me feel as if I were part of Europe.

After the lemon mousse, my mother-in-law brought in little cups of coffee and served liqueurs.

"If you'll excuse me, I think I'll get dressed," I said, standing up.

"I'll come and help you," Emma said. She had not missed my signal. We went upstairs to the guest room. Emma shut the door behind us and then pushed me toward my new clothes.

This was my wedding day. All over town people were getting dressed up. At ten to three the bells would begin to ring, and curious children would gather in front of the church, wanting to see me, the bride, and wait for the sugar candy that would be thrown to them. I would walk down the aisle, holding my father's arm, my long white veil not quite hiding my apprehension. Peter and the minister would be waiting for me at the altar. I would listen to the words, try to follow them, and at the right time I would say, "oui." Yes, yes, I wanted to be married.

There was a knock on the door. It was my father.

"May I come in?" He looked so handsome, his moustache trimmed to follow his upper lip.

"Emma, do you mind? Dianne and I won't have any time to be together after the wedding. I'm taking the plane back to San Francisco tomorrow morning."

"Of course not. She's ready. Doesn't she look splendid?" Emma said, gathering up her mascara, which she had been putting on my eyelashes.

Daddy stood in the middle of the room without really looking at me and held his hands in a tight knot. I recognized the signs. He wanted to speak seriously. I wondered if he was going to get angry. We had only spent a few hours together since he had arrived, and most of that time I had been an interpreter since my father spoke only English and Peter and his parents did not always understand him.

I tried to stay composed, but I felt guilty. My parents had sent me to Switzerland, offering me a year of cosmopolitan schooling, before I started university. I had never accepted our immigration to the United States because I thought that we had lived more happily in New Zealand. Europe was supposed to give me a broader view of life. My father had not counted on my becoming a pregnant teenager.

"Peter seems a very stable young man," Daddy began. I picked up his conciliatory tone and expanded on it.

"His company is sending him to the States soon — for a year. He's crazy about Americans."   ·

"I know, dear. We've been talking." I fell silent, but I was pleased that my father was taking my marriage so well.

"Your mother and I will arrange to have your books and things shipped when I get home. It might take some time because they'll have to go around the Horn, but, as far as I can see, your new family will make sure you have everything you need."

As my father talked, I felt a surge of loss. I pushed the feeling away.

"You always wanted to return to New Zealand. Oh dear, I guess I'm having a bit of trouble adjusting to my daughter's new role. So many changes." I saw my father's mouth tremble, and I wanted to touch him but was afraid he would cry. I had never seen my father in tears, and I couldn't handle his emotion as well as my own. It didn't take long, though, for him to straighten up.

"I am sorry about your studies though. You mustn't stop. You're too intelligent. Maybe you can go back to them after the baby's born. Anyway, I'm sure that you can work something out."

At that moment I felt myself to be floundering. My father was pulling out, and my mother would follow him. Of course, Peter and his parents would take good care of me. I was one of them now. For the first time I admitted it. But the Swiss did not encourage young wives to go back to school. Their place was at home. My father was telling me to be courageous and face my destiny. My family had been perennial immigrants for several generations, and I knew the refrain. I had chosen my way, and it was up to me to follow it successfully.

"You're going to learn French and German easily," he continued. I nodded. There was nothing I could say. He went on. Already his voice seemed to come from some inaccessible place.

"I know how much you love reading, and the English language has always been your thing. I thought you'd like this. It's my wedding gift."

In his hand was a package which he held out to me. I took it and undid the ribbon. Inside was *The Complete Works of Shakespeare.* My fingers caressed the leather binding. I was giving up so much, going so far away, and he was leaving me with poetry as an open passage to my past. I turned to the first page. In my father's handwriting I read: "To a darling daughter on a very special visit to Switzerland. January 1964."

AUCKLAND, NEW ZEALAND — APRIL 1985

The early morning sun tickled my eyelids, but I was not ready to open my eyes. It was pure joy to let sleep drift away. I had spent so many years waking to duty, trying to fit into a role that did not suit me, that I had forgotten the euphoria of a new day. A bellbird sang. Each note rolled in my ears, and its echo shook me. My flight was due to leave in the late evening. I lay still, remembering.

For my fortieth birthday Peter had offered me a holiday in New Zealand. Alone. He said it was too far for him. The day after I stepped out of the plane into the vibrant Pacific air, I had met Alistair. A Swiss friend had asked me to look him up. Could I drop him off some chocolates? He came toward my car as if he had been waiting for me.

With Alistair, I set a part of myself loose that had been constrained for over twenty years. I knew when that constraint had begun. It was when I signed my husband's name to a piece of paper. I had signed away my freedom without even knowing it was mine.

Peter expected me to adapt to his lifestyle before I was experienced enough to know who I was or what I wanted. Eager to please, I became a traditional wife and mother, trying to copy the practical efficiency I observed in my mother-in-law. I drifted in my husband's shadow, disconsolate because I felt no one understood me. My tears and my anger seemed to leave no trace on Peter. He thought that I was just more complicated than most women and, along with his parents, he believed that my childhood was to blame. With time I would calm down.

"Tell me what you are thinking." Alistair's gentle voice interrupted my thoughts. I kept my eyes closed as he touched my nose, my cheeks, my lips.

"You will always be beautiful." I opened my eyes. The bellbird had finished its song.

With Alistair my life went all the way back to its beginning. Our language was the same; I could leave sentences unfinished, and I was understood. His childhood was like mine, because we both came from colonial families and had grown up in boarding schools. Alistair wanted to know my desires, but he quickly discovered that I did not know them myself.

I got out of bed and walked over to the open window. Long lines of kiwi vines, heavy with furry oval fruit, stretched out in front of me. It would soon be time to harvest. Beyond the orchard I could see the sparkle of waves as they curled over and caught the sunlight. To the left, a wind barrier of poplar trees already tinted yellow stood stiff and straight as dinner forks. I turned back to Alistair.

"I seem to have mucked up everything," I said to him.

"Not really. You're just finding out who you are." He looked through me as if I had already gone. I wanted to shake him. His features took on the absent, concentrated expression of a child who has just begun to realize the importance of memories.

"Do you remember when you spent that first night here? I was afraid of being hurt, but I was so flattered by your attention. I thought you were some European sophisticate."

"I hoped you would save me." I felt his bereavement as I felt my own.

"No regrets?"

"No, Alistair, none. But let's leave it like that."

He got out of bed and went into the bathroom. I heard him turn on the shower. I glanced at my suitcase, packed but still open. Alistair had placed my journal on the top. I reached over and picked it up. He had filled in several pages in neat flowing handwriting. I would read it later.

Ever since I was a child, I had kept a journal but had never shared it with anyone. Alistair was the first person who showed any interest in my writing. He understood that I communicated most easily that way. Writing grounded me. When he began to read, I felt terrified of exposure but also relieved. At last I was taken seriously. My husband had ignored my journal, and I felt uncomfortable sharing any feelings with him. He seemed so self-contained. We had so little trust in each other. I belonged to him, and he was obligated to care for me. A part of him must have resented the responsibility.

I knew how firm my husband was whenever principles were concerned, and the Calvinist environment in which we lived re-inforced his feelings of righteousness. But after I wrote to Peter, telling him about Alistair, he surprised me. He replied, without anger or jealousy, saying only that he loved me and would wait for me.

Alistair came out of the bathroom. He looked at the journal and then at me.

"It's good. You have something to say. Keep going."

"I'm going to try," I said, recalling my father's wedding present. He, too, believed I had a special relationship with my mother tongue.

"There's something I want to ask you," I went on hesitantly.

"Hmm?"

"Do you think I'm going backwards if I return to Peter?"

"I don't think that's for me to say."

"You see, I've run away. My marriage is still sunk in silence. Peter and I need to talk, and I don't even know whether we can. I always felt he knew better. You know the Swiss impress me. They're so reasonable." I laughed, uneasy with my excuses and with Alistair's quiet presence. At forty I was still justifying myself like a schoolgirl.

"I guess I was foolish. I have my place in Switzerland and in my family. But it's only now that I feel strong enough to say it." I stopped speaking and put my journal back in the suitcase. Then I turned to him.

"I owe you so much . . ."

"Shhhhhh."

I knew the last day I spent on Alistair's farm would leave a permanent imprint on my mind. I stayed outside and wandered in the fields and the orchard, immersed in familiarity, until I felt every blade of grass and every cloud had blessed me.

The smell of seaweed abandoned by the tide on a nearby beach and the sounds of cattle herding around the water trough intensified my kaleidoscope of pleasures. My senses had reawakened. I was at home as I had not been in thirty years.

Later, as I wandered down the lanes of pregnant kiwi vines, I thought of Alistair. He represented everything that was good about my past. Then I brooded over Peter. I longed to hug and kiss our children, and I wondered how I could feel all of these loves at the same time.

With Alistair I had learned that I had only exchanged one man's house for another when I got married. The solution to my frustration and unhappiness was not in my choice of partner. I wanted self-knowledge. As a child I had gone from an island paradise to an American immigrant dream. At eighteen, afraid of facing solitude, I had settled for conventional security. The price was high. In Switzerland when I married, women did not exist outside of their homes and families. For twenty years I persisted, using my children as an excuse to remain safe. Now my children were almost adults, and my husband seemed a stranger. I wanted to know him again on another level, but what were my personal needs? I had decisions to make over work and finances. I also needed to find my own values.

I walked under a canopy of leaves, my feet squelching the ripe fruit that had fallen to the ground. I took off my shoes. The green pulp oozed up between my toes. I imagined that I could lick it the way an animal licks a festering wound in order to heal it. Instead, I kept on walking. The autumn sun receded and shadows stretched across the vines. I headed back to the house. Through an incision, opened deliberately, New Zealand had entered my very marrow.

Alistair prepared lamb chops, and we had a bottle of local wine. We ate and drank slowly at a table by the kitchen window and tasted sadness in every mouthful. Afterwards, I checked the bedroom before I closed my suitcase. As I turned out the light, I noticed the crumpled blue sheets. Alistair would change them tomorrow.

The line at the check-in counter at Auckland airport was long. I waited, clutching my ticket and my New Zealand passport. My Swiss passport lay in my suitcase. I could bring it out again when I went back to Switzerland. It did not matter which one I used. Like the two hemispheres, my nationalities complimented one another and made up my identity.

"I don't want you to wait," I said again to Alistair, who stood beside me.

"Just let me make sure about your seat. Then I'll go."

It was my turn. The plane was full and the choice of seats was limited. I did not care. To cross the world in thirty hours in any available armchair was pretty good to me. I took my boarding card and turned away.

"So this is good-bye," I said, wondering how I could stand it. Alistair closed his arms around me.

"Thank you for everything."

"No letters, just trust better things lie ahead for both of us."

We kissed. Alistair lowered his arms, then stepped back, turned around, and walked away. I watched him as he made his way through the crowd of excited travellers. He passed through the sliding doors and disappeared into the night.

I stayed a while staring at the space where he had stood. I could feel the seconds tick by. I was almost paralyzed. It seemed impossible, but I moved over to passport control. Inside I could hear myself screaming, but the man at the desk just smiled and wished me a pleasant flight.

Once inside the waiting room, I found a corner seat and sat down. There remained another twenty minutes before my plane would be called. I put my hands on my knees, afraid to see them trembling. The pain was so profound that even tears could not reach it, but with a shudder, I let it flow through me. I felt almost flooded with it, but I was determined to be responsible. I could live with loss; I would not drown.

Then a new sensation washed over me. I felt intense joy. How could I dare be like this? I had trouble naming it, but the happiness was there along with the distress that the separation from Alistair had stirred up in me. I was no longer frightened. I alone was responsible for my life. My well-being had nothing to do with being married or single, or with nationalities, religions, or languages. It had nothing to do with any exterior force or person. It had only to do with me.

I took a deep breath.

I knew then that returning to Peter was the right choice. We still had the possibility of loving one another. If we really wanted our marriage to work, then we would learn to speak about our problems just like any other couple. Maybe we did have three languages to deal with, instead of only one, but that made our marriage richer. The same could be said about all the other differences. It was a matter of attitude. We had already overcome so many difficulties in our youths, and now Peter had risen above his background and had accepted my adultery. He knew that I wanted to be more than just his wife and mother to our children. I appreciated his capacity to evolve and his unselfish attitude. I felt unaccustomed solidarity with and tenderness toward him.

"Air New Zealand, for Honolulu, Los Angeles, London will now begin boarding," the loudspeaker announced. Passengers picked up bags and raincoats. Children ran to their parents, and an elderly woman was pushed forward in a wheelchair. The doors were opened, and one by one we handed over our boarding cards. I did not have any hand luggage, just my budding self-confidence. It was all I needed.

MYSELF
IN
INDIA

Ruth Prawer-Jhabvala

 have lived in India for most of my adult life. My husband is Indian and so are my children. I am not, and less so every year.

People react very strongly to India. Some loathe it, some love it, most do both. There is a special problem of adjustment for the sort of people who come today, who tend to be liberal in outlook and have been educated to be sensitive and receptive to other cultures. But it is not always easy to be sensitive and receptive to India: there comes a point where you have to close up in order to protect yourself. The place is very strong and often proves too strong for European nerves. There is a cycle that Europeans—by Europeans I mean all Westerners, including Americans—tend to pass through. It goes like this: first stage, tremendous enthusiasm — everything Indian is marvelous; second stage, everything Indian not so marvelous; third stage, everything Indian abominable. For some people it ends there, for others the cycle renews itself and goes on. I have been through it so many times that now I think of myself as strapped to a wheel that goes round and round and sometimes I'm up and sometimes I'm down. When I meet other Europeans, I can usually tell after a few moments' conversation at what stage of the cycle they happen to be. Everyone likes to talk about India, whether they happen to be loving or loathing it. It is a topic on which a lot of things can be said, and on a variety of aspects — social, economic, political, philosophical: it makes fascinating viewing from every side.

However, I must admit that I am no longer interested in India. What I am interested in now is myself in India — which sometimes, in moments of despondency, I tend to think of as my survival in India. I had better say straightaway that the reason I live in India is that my strongest human ties are here. If I hadn't married an Indian, I don't think I would ever have come here, for I am not attracted — or used not to be attracted — to the things that usually bring people to India. I know I am the wrong type of person to live here. To stay and endure, one should have a mission and a cause, to be patient, cheerful, unselfish, strong. I am a central European with an English education and a deplorable tendency to constant self-analysis. I am irritable and have weak nerves.

The most salient fact about India is that it is very poor and very backward. There are so many other things to be said about it, but this must remain the basis of all of them. We may praise Indian democracy, go into raptures over Indian music, admire Indian intellectuals — but whatever we say, not for one moment should we lose sight of the fact that a very great number of Indians never get enough to eat. Literally that: from birth to death they never for one day cease to suffer from hunger. *Can* one lose sight of that fact? God knows, I've tried. But after seeing what one has to see here every day, it is not really possible to go on living one's life the way one is used to. People dying of starvation in the streets, children kidnapped and maimed to be sent out as beggars — but there is no point in making a catalog of the horrors with which one lives, *on* which one lives, as on the back of an animal. Obviously, there has to be some adjustment.

There are several ways. The first and best is to be a strong person who plunges in and does what he can as a doctor or social worker. I often think that perhaps this is the only condition under which Europeans have any right to be here. I know several people like that. They are usually attached to some mission. They work very hard and stay very cheerful. Every few years they are sent on home leave. Once I met such a person — a woman doctor — who had just returned from her first home leave after being out here for twelve years. I asked her: but what does it feel like to go back after such a long time? How do you manage to adapt yourself? She didn't understand. This question, which was of such tremendous import to me — how to adapt oneself to the differences between Europe and India — didn't mean a thing to her. It simply didn't matter. And she was right, for in view of the things she sees and does every day, the delicate nuances of one's own sensibilities are best forgotten.

Another approach to India's basic conditions is to accept them. This seems to be the approach favored by most Indians. Perhaps it has something to do with their belief in reincarnation. If things are not to your liking in this life, there is always the chance that in your next life everything will be different. It appears to be a consoling thought for both rich and poor. The rich man stuffing himself on the pilau can do so with an easy conscience because he knows he has earned this privilege by his good conduct in previous lives; and the poor man can watch him with some degree of equanimity, for he knows that next time around it may well be *he* who will be digging into that pilau, while the other will be crouching outside the door with an empty stomach. However, this path of acceptance is not open to you if you don't have a belief in reincarnation ingrained within you. And if you don't accept, then what can you do? Sometimes one wants just to run away and go to a place where everyone has enough to eat and clothes to wear and a home fit to live in. But even when you get there, can you ever forget? Having once seen the sights in India, and the way it has been ordained that people must live out their lives, nowhere in the world can ever be all that good to be in again.

None of this is what I wanted to say. I wanted to concentrate only on myself in India. But I could not do so before indicating the basis on which everyone who comes here has to live. I have a nice house, I do my best to live in an agreeable way. I shut all my windows, I let down the blinds, I turn on the air-conditioner; I read a lot of books, with a special preference for the great masters of the novel. All the time I know myself to be on the back of this great animal of poverty and backwardness. It is not possible to pretend otherwise. Or rather, one does pretend, but retribution follows. Even if one never rolls up the blinds and never turns off the air-conditioner, something is bound to go wrong. People are not meant to shut themselves up in rooms and pretend there is nothing outside.

Now I think I am drawing nearer to what I want to be my subject. Yes, something is wrong: I am not happy this way. I feel lonely, shut in, shut off. It is my own fault. I should go out more and meet people and learn what is going on. All right, so I am not a doctor or a social worker or a saint or at all a good person; then the only thing to do is to try to push that aspect of India out of sight and turn to others. There are many others. I live in the capital, where so much is going on. The winter is one round of parties, art exhibitions, plays, music and dance recitals, visiting European artists: there need never be a dull moment. Yet all my moments are dull. Why? It is my own fault, I know. I can't quite explain it to myself, but somehow I have no heart for these things here. Is it because all the time underneath I feel the animal moving? But I have decided to ignore the animal. I wish to concentrate only on modern, Westernized India, and on modern, well-off, cultured Westernized Indians.

Let me try and describe a Westernized Indian woman with whom I ought to have a lot in common and whose company I ought to enjoy. She has been to Oxford or Cambridge or some smart American college. She speaks flawless, easy, colloquial English with a charming lilt of an accent. She has a degree in economics or political science or English literature. She comes from a good family. Her father may have been an I.C.S. officer or some other high-ranking government official; he too was at Oxford or Cambridge, and he and her mother traveled in Europe in prewar days. They have always lived a Western-style life, with Western food and an admiration for Western culture. The daughter now tends rather to frown on this. She feels one should be more deeply Indian, and with this end in view, she wears handloom saris and traditional jewelry and has painted an abnormally large vermilion mark on her forehead. She is interested in Indian classical music and dance. If she is rich enough—she may have married into one of the big Indian business houses—she will become a patroness of the arts and hold delicious parties on her lawn on summer nights. All her friends are there—and she has so many, both Indian and European, all interesting people—and trays of iced drinks are carried around by servants in uniform and there is intelligent conversation and then there is a superbly arranged buffet supper and more intelligent conversation, and then the crown of the evening: a famous Indian maestro performing on the sitar. The guests recline on carpets and cushions on the lawn. The sky sparkles with stars and the languid summer air is fragrant with jasmine. There are many pretty girls reclining against bolsters; their faces are melancholy, for the music is stirring their hearts, and sometimes they sigh with yearning and happiness and look down at their pretty toes (adorned with a tiny silver toe ring) peeping out from under the sari. Here is Indian life and culture at its highest and best. Yet, with all that, it need not be thought that our hostess has forgotten her Western education. Not at all. In her one may see the best of East and West combined. She is interested in a great variety of topics and can hold her own in any discussion. She loves to exercise her emancipated mind, and whatever the subject of conversation — economics or politics or literature or film — she has a well-formulated opinion on it and knows how to express herself. How lucky for me if I could have such a person for a friend! What enjoyable, lively times we two could have together!

In fact, my teeth are set on edge if I have to listen to her for more than five minutes — yes, even though everything she says is so true and in line with the most advanced opinions of today. But when she says it, somehow, even though I know the words to be true, they ring completely false. It is merely lips moving and sounds coming out: it doesn't mean anything, nothing of what she says (though she says it with such conviction, skill, and charm) is one of the least importance to her. She is only making conversation in the way she knows educated women have to make conversation. And so it is with all of them. Everything they say, all that lively conversation around the buffet table, is not prompted by anything they really feel strongly about but by what they think they ought to feel strongly about. This applies not only to subjects that are naturally alien to them — for instance, when they talk oh so solemnly! and with such profound intelligence! of Godard and Beckett and ecology — but when they talk about themselves too. They know modern India to be an important subject and they have a lot to say about it: but though they themselves *are* modern India, they don't look at themselves, they are not conditioned to look at themselves except with the eyes of foreign experts whom they have been taught to respect. And while they are fully aware of India's problems and are up on all the statistics and all the arguments for and against nationalization and a socialistic pattern of society, all the time it is as if they were talking about some *other* place — as if it were a subject for debate — an abstract subject — and not a live animal actually moving under their feet.

But if I have no taste for the company of these Westernized Indians, then what else is there? Other Indians don't really have a social life, not in our terms; the whole conception of such a life is imported. It is true that Indians are gregarious insofar as they hate to be alone and always like to sit together in groups; but these groups are clan-units — it is the family, or clan members, who gather together and enjoy each other's company. And again, their conception of enjoying each other's company is different from ours. For them it is enough just to *be* together; there are long stretches of silence in which everyone stares into space. From time to time there is a little spurt of conversation, usually on some commonplace everyday subject such as rising prices, a forthcoming marriage, or a troublesome neighbor. There is no attempt at exercising the mind or testing one's wits against those of others: the pleasure lies only in having other familiar people around and enjoying the air together and looking forward to the next meal. There is actually something very restful about this mode of social intercourse, and it certainly holds more pleasure than the synthetic social life led by Westernized Indians. It is also more adapted to the Indian climate, which invites one to be absolutely relaxed in mind and body, to do nothing, to think nothing, just to feel, to *be*. I have in fact enjoyed sitting around like that for hours on end. But there is something in me that after some time revolts against such lassitude. I can't just *be*! Suddenly I jump up and rush away out of that contented circle. I want to do something terribly difficult like climbing a mountain or reading the *Critique of Pure Reason*. I feel tempted to bang my head against the wall as if to wake myself up. Anything to prevent myself from being sucked down into that bog of passive, intuitive being. I feel I cannot, I must not allow myself to live this way.

Of course there are other Europeans more or less in the same situation as myself. For instance, other women married to Indians. But I hesitate to seek them out. People suffering from the same disease do not usually make good company for one another. Who is to listen to whose complaints? On the other hand, with what enthusiasm I welcome visitors from abroad. Their physical presence alone is a pleasure to me. I love to see their fresh complexions, their red cheeks that speak of wind and rain; and I like to see their clothes and their shoes, to admire the texture of these solid European materials and their industrial skills that have gone into making them. I also like to hear the way in which these people speak. In some strange way their accents, their intonations are redolent to me of the places from which they have come, so that as voices rise and fall I hear in them the wind stirring in English trees or a mild brook murmuring through a summer wood. And apart from these sensuous pleasures, there is also the pleasure of hearing what they have to say. I listen avidly to what is said about people I know or have heard of and about new plays and restaurants and changes and fashions. However, neither the subject nor my interest in it is inexhaustible; and after that, it is my turn. What about India? Now they want to hear, but I don't want to say. I feel myself growing sullen. I don't want to talk about India. There is nothing I can tell them. There is nothing they would understand. However, I do begin to talk, and after a time even to talk with passion. But everything I say is wrong. I listen to myself with horror; they too listen with horror. I want to stop and reverse, but I can't. I want to cry out, this is not what I mean! You are listening to me in entirely the wrong context! But there is no way of explaining the context. It would take too long, and anyway what is the point? It's such a small, personal thing. I fall silent. I have nothing more to say. I turn my face and want them to go away.

So I am back again alone in my room with the blinds drawn and the air conditioner on. Sometimes, when I think of my life, it seems to have contracted to this one point and to be concentrated in this one room, and it is always a very hot, very long afternoon when the air-conditioner has failed. I cannot describe the *oppression* of such afternoons. It is a physical oppression — heat pressing down on me and pressing in the walls and the ceiling and congealing together with time that has stood still and will never move again. And it is not only those two — heat and time — that are laying their weight on me but behind them, or held within them, there is something more, which I can only describe as the whole of India. This is hyperbole, but I need hyperbole to express my feelings about those countless afternoons spent over what now seem to be countless years in a country for which I was not born. India swallows me up and now it seems to me that I am no longer in my room but in the white-hot city streets under a white-hot sky; people cannot live in such heat, so everything is deserted — no, not quite, for here comes a smiling leper in a cart being pushed by another leper; there is also a carcass of a dog and vultures have swooped down on it. The river has dried up and stretches in miles of flat cracked earth; it is not possible to make out where the river ceases and the land begins, for this too is flat, as cracked, as dry as the riverbed and stretches on forever. Until we come to a jungle in which wild beasts live, and then there are ravines and here live outlaws with the hearts of wild beasts. Sometimes they make raids into the villages, and they rob and burn and mutilate and kill for sport. More mountains and these are very, very high, and now it is no longer hot but terribly cold, we are in snow and ice and here is Mount Kailash on which sits Siva the Destroyer wearing a necklace of human skulls. Down in the plains they are worshipping him. I can see them from here — they are doing something strange — what is it? I draw nearer. Now I can see. They are killing a boy. They hack him to pieces, and now they bury the pieces in the foundations dug for a new bridge. There is a priest with them who is quite naked except for ash smeared all over him; he is reciting some holy verses over the foundations, to bless and propitiate.

I am using these exaggerated images in order to give some idea of how intolerable India — the idea, the sensation of it — can become. A point is reached where one must escape, and if one can't do so physically, then some other way must be found. And I think it is not only Europeans but Indians too who feel themselves compelled to seek refuge from their often unbearable environment. Here perhaps less than anywhere else is it possible to believe that this world, this life, is all there is for us, and the temptation to write it off and substitute something more satisfying becomes overwhelming. This brings up the question of whether religion is such a potent force in India because life is so terrible, or is it the other way around—is life so terrible because, with the eyes of the spirit turned elsewhere, there is no incentive to improve its quality? Whichever it is, the fact remains that the eyes of the spirit *are* turned elsewhere, and it really is true that God seems more present in India than in other places. Every morning I wake up at 3 A.M. to the sound of someone pouring out his spirit in devotional song; and then at dawn the temple bells ring, and again at dusk, and conch shells are blown, and there is the smell of incense and of the slightly overblown flowers that are placed at the feet of smiling, pink-cheeked idols. I read in the papers that the Lord Krishna has been reborn as the son of a weaver woman in a village somewhere in Madhya Pradesh. On the banks of the river there are figures in meditation, and one of them may turn out to be the teller in your bank who cashed your check just a few days ago; now he is in the lotus pose, and his eyes are turned up and he is in ecstasy. There are ashrams full of little old half-starved widows who skip and dance about, they giggle and play hide-and-seek because they are Krishna's milkmaids. And over all this there is a sky of enormous proportions—so much larger than the earth on which you live, and often so incredibly beautiful, that it is difficult to believe that something grand and wonderful beyond the bounds of human comprehension does not emanate from there.

I love listening to Indian devotional songs. They seem pure like water drawn from a well; and the emotions they express are both beautiful and easy to understand because the imagery employed is so human. The soul crying out for God is always shown as the beloved yearning for the lover in an easily recognizable way ("I wait for Him. Do you hear His step? He has come"). I feel soothed when I hear such songs and all my discontentment falls away. I see that everything I have been fretting about is of no importance at all because all that matters is this promise of eternal bliss in the Lover's arms. I become patient and good and feel that everything is good. Unfortunately this tranquil state does not last for long, and after a time it again seems to me that nothing is good and neither am I. Once somebody said to me: "Just see, how sweet is the Indian soul that can see God in a cow!" But when I try to assume this sweetness, it turns sour: for, however much I may try to fool myself, whatever veils I may try for the sake of peace of mind to draw over my eyes, it is soon enough clear to me that the cow *is* a cow, and a very scrawny, underfed, diseased one at that. And then I feel that I want to keep this knowledge, however painful it is, and not exchange it for some other that may be true for an Indian but can never quite become that for me.

And here, it seems to me, I come to the heart of my problem. To live in India and be at peace, one must to a very considerable extent become an Indian and adopt Indian attitudes, habits, beliefs, assume if possible an Indian personality. But how is this possible? And even if it were possible — without cheating oneself — would it be desirable? Should one want to try to become something other than what one is? I don't always say no to this question. Sometimes it seems to me how pleasant it would be to say yes and give in and wear a sari and be meek and accepting and see God in a cow. Other times it seems worthwhile to be defiant and European and — all right, be crushed by one's environment, but all the same have made some attempt to remain standing. Of course, this can't go on indefinitely, and in the end I'm bound to lose — if only at the point where my ashes are immersed in the Ganges to the accompaniment of Vedic hymns, and then who will say that I have not truly merged with India?

I do sometimes go back to Europe. But after a time I get bored there and want to come back here. I also find it hard now to stand the European climate. I have got used to intense heat and seem to need it.

CROSSING CULTURES: THE STORY OF A CHINESE MAN AND AN AMERICAN WOMAN

Nora Egan

he Chinese university spread out on a gently sloping hill with classical Chinese buildings looking like Spanish villas along either side of a wide walkway. At night, lit by ground-level lamps, it had the atmosphere of another century. Dark-tiled roofs and tall windows overlooked the four-sided courtyards and covered walkways. The winds pushed through the windows during class, flies buzzed, and bamboo leaves rustled amid the terse phrases of Chinese lectures.

SEPTEMBER 1979

Taiwan. Junior Year Abroad. I had started studying Chinese to learn what this oldest continuous civilization knew about life. Only a year later, I found myself rooming with five Chinese women in the women's dormitories, taking a full set of classes in Chinese. The island of Taiwan was tropical, lush and beautiful. My American classmates were intelligent and imaginative. My Chinese classes excited me, opening my mind to worlds unknown to people who could not see through the Chinese language. There were many late nights peeling away layers of distractions in my thoughts to open my memory to the dozens of new Chinese characters I had to learn each day. I felt exhilarated being in such a foreign land, but it was also traumatic.

Everywhere I went I was seen. In the daylight there was nowhere I could escape my foreignness, nowhere I dared to go at night and feel safe. It was like being boxed in, being trapped on center stage. Strangely, despite being constantly surrounded by people, there was an intense isolation that weighed on me like the heavy humid air of the summer or the damp cold of winter. My favorite Chinese word was *chi ji* or "knowing the self": the word for an intimate friend, one who knew one's self. I longed for a *chi ji*.

My communication was reduced to children's sentences. It was as if I had become physically impaired; my mind raced with ideas and observations, but I couldn't get them out. To compensate, all my expressiveness shifted to my face and hands. I was humbled. Never again would I judge people by how articulate they were, for underneath a simple or silent expression could be a vast and deep realm of experience and feeling.

SPRING 1980

Taiwan. I was standing in the post office by the counter checking for letters in the small foreign-student mailboxes. I became aware of a tall, slim man beside me at the mail counter; I looked up. There stood a handsome, broad-faced Chinese man, dressed in a formal navy suit, with envelopes to American universities in his hand. I watched as he shuffled through the envelopes. There it was, on the last one, my university, the school I would return to in September.

In a flash, an instant that felt like lightning, my mind raced ahead: he'll go to my school, we'll fall in love and marry. I glanced again, looking for a wedding ring. None. But he looked older, surely he was married and with children. I walked away.

SEPTEMBER 1980

New England. Hot. Tall green oaks towering over small country roads in an elegant town along the Connecticut river. I had moved into a student-occupied apartment complex among to-bacco fields. I roomed with a close friend who had studied in Taiwan with me. After living in spartan rooms with five Chinese roommates, we found these bare U.S. apartments had every-thing we needed: hot water, a stove, heating, a view over fields, a bus to the university, and, most precious of all, privacy.

One Saturday we walked over to the laundromat. There was our Chinese teaching assistant from the year before. He excit-edly asked about our year in Taiwan, and then, just before leav-ing, introduced us to a tall, lanky Chinese man from the univer-sity we had just returned from.

This newcomer was astonished that my roommate and I could speak Mandarin so well. He thought he might have seen us before, but I had no recollection of ever having seen him. We chatted excitedly, exchanged a variety of details, including, con-veniently, that my roommate was married and I was not. We in-vited him over for tea some afternoon. As we walked back to our second-floor flat, my roommate remarked, "He likes you." I was embarrassed.

Seeing him at the bus stop later that week, we again invited him for tea. My roommate and I had been introduced to the art of Chinese teas. I had a precious, brown terra-cotta, miniature Chinese tea set, in which the finest teas are steeped for tea connoisseurs, and we had with us some excellent Tong Ting Ou Long Ch'a (Eastern Peak Black Dragon Tea), which leaves a subtle aromatic flavor on the palate after going down. He, an avid tea drinker, was visibly delighted.

As I saw him over the next weeks, I could not believe the struggles he faced adjusting to life in a competitive M.B.A. program in a language that was not his own. I identified so much with being overwhelmed. Instinctively, I wanted to help, almost as if by helping him I was erasing the terrible isolation I had felt through the year before. But little did I know, little did I realize, what my kindness was inviting.

It wasn't long before he asked for help on his business cases. I asked for help pronouncing the Chinese characters in the classical Chinese poetry I was studying. Looking up Chinese characters in a dictionary required immense patience counting out each of the strokes (some less evident than others) and then looking through the collection of characters with the same stroke count in the dictionary. By contrast, if one knew the pronunciation, one could look up the character in the index by sound, a much quicker process. Our partnership was established.

He recorded the Chinese poems for me so I could look up the meanings word by word. I rewrote and typed his business cases, learning about business, pleased that I had something to offer. I baked a cornbread and invited him over to have some. He made egg custard and cooked Chinese beef noodles and invited me over. It speaks of the loneliness and isolation I had felt in my life, despite a very close friend in my roommate, that in this barren apartment with old broken furniture, I felt enormous comfort from this offer of food and sharing. It filled a vacuum.

I experienced an entirely different kind of caring through him, not one of flowers, cards, and holding hands, but one of tangible caring for my warmth, my health, and my well-being. He gave me rubber gloves for washing dishes at the sink so that my hands would not get rough. It moved me deeply.

One night he sat me down in the kitchen and talked about

my future, how I would earn my living, where I would go, how to put my languages and background to use. My parents were overseas. No aunts or uncles around. No one to guide me — not that I accepted guidance from anyone! This interest in my rudderless life in my senior year of university felt like tender care.

Over time, it became clear that he was interested, and while I had not yet admitted it, I was interested, too. Still, I kept my distance, unaware that my kindness was promoting his interest. I was haunted. At once drawn by his almond-shaped eyes and fine skin, the gentle ways of caring through food and discussion, and all the wisdom embodied in an educated Chinese family still carrying on traditions from old, but very scared of crossing races and cultures and languages. His father was a calligrapher. He wore a long navy robe and rubbed an ink stick on ink stone to do exquisite Chinese calligraphy in all its forms. I was enchanted.

One day in a university lecture hall, I heard an engaging talk by an anthropologist. I sought her counsel afterwards. I asked about crossing the great cultural divide, living on the bridge between two cultures. We talked at length and on several occasions. With encouragement that it could work, I dared to consider it.

One evening as he came closer to me and I drew away, as I always did, admonishing that it is better to let a fire burn slowly and last long than to burn quickly, I realized the allure was growing stronger than my rational caution. I pulled back. "I can't get involved, you are Chinese." But this time, with words whose power he could not have known, he reached my heart. He replied in Chinese, "But, I, too, am human."

We spent a lot of time together that year. He asked whether I could consider marriage. I was not ready, but I wanted to stay in the relationship. Not knowing what to do upon graduation, I jumped at the opportunity to go to China on another exchange program. In August 1981 I boarded a plane for Hong Kong, destination Beijing, China.

JANUARY 1982

Chinese New Year. A classmate and I took the two-and-a-half-day train ride from Beijing to Hong Kong and out of the People's Republic of China. We flew separately to Taiwan to meet our boyfriends and their families.

I had virtually no clothes with me, just baggy navy blue pants and tops that kept me as unnoticeable as a foreigner could be in mainland China. My mother had sent me some of her clothes along with a gift for his parents, and some money to make the trip possible. So much weighed on this trip. I even bought special Chinese medicine for his mother, costing over one hundred dollars. As I passed through Taiwanese customs, my heart pounded so terribly that I felt as if it was jumping out of my chest. I offered my second passport free of all People's Republic of China visas. The officers opened my luggage—would they find the medicine? Would there be trouble for me, having come from Communist China? But they did not see the Chinese products. With praise for my spoken Chinese, they waved me through, and I got a room in the International Student Center.

For our first meeting, he came to pick me up at the Center. Dressed in my mother's beige pants, with black plastic sandals that passed for leather purchased at an open-air market in Hong Kong, we climbed the stairs to the apartment and started to take off our shoes. His parents opened the door. I could hardly breathe. I could hardly feel anything. How does one do things like this, going to meet the parents of such a foreigner? The stress was unbearable.

Across the threshold I saw two warm faces and heard, as if through a long distance monitor, welcoming voices, saying, *Huan ying. Huan ying.* "Welcome. Welcome." Hands were extended. Smiles offered. I was shown a seat. Everywhere along the living room walls were calligraphy scrolls, and the exquisite Hsu Pei-Hong–style horses that were so famous a couple of generations ago.

His father was slim and dressed in a business suit, very energetic, upbeat with sparkling eyes. His mother was gentle, with a full, generous smile, but weary. Into the kitchen she went. I offered to help but was asked to sit. I looked to him for confirmation as to what I should do. He nodded his head. I sat awkwardly but still. I watched as he put his arm around his mother, ever so gently patted her on the back, and quietly asked if he could help at all. I watched the way one would watch a captor come to the door with a key, watching to see if it would open for me. He was tender, affectionate, and caring. I saw this gesture and read into it all the love and respect and support that I would want from a man.

In this one moment I made my decision. It had been a year and a half since we met, and one year since he had first brought up the question of marriage. It was something I had not even thought of but began ever so hesitantly considering. In this one moment's tenderness between a son and his mother, I felt I could trust him. This man had cultivation, manners, and love. He was intelligent and he had the willingness to work hard. He was also outgoing and sociable. I could marry this man.

Only many years later would I remember this moment and realize all that I had not seen — that although the love and respect for his mother were indeed there, so was the clear knowledge of what her work was, and what his work was, and that only in exceptional circumstances would that cross. I did not notice that neither he nor his father actually helped. I did not know that she would not have asked for help, and that in fact she would refuse help. I did not see this, in this one moment that determined so much for my future.

His father talked attentively with me, asking after my family, and China. The TV news showed scenes from around the world, with a lot from America. It reminded me how far from home I was. Every few minutes another dish of steaming food arrived on the round table: colorful vegetables, meats, and seafoods. Finally, we were called to the table. His father and mother each said a few words of welcome. I was asked whether I needed a fork. I shook my head, picked up the chopsticks, and we began to eat. I praised the exceptionally good food. I offered to help with dishes. His mother emphatically refused, so I sat in the living room. We were served refreshing sliced oranges. Before long, he showed me to the door and sent me home by cab.

The next day, we met at a park and walked side by side along a lotus-filled pond. The air was warm, and many couples sat affectionately on the park benches. As a biracial couple, we did not show any outward sign of affection: it would draw too much attention to us. As it was, people's heads turned just because we were together, a Chinese man and an American woman.

Sitting at the bus stop to go to his parents' for dinner, he asked me to wipe his glasses. He took them off and handed them to me. I was startled. I couldn't understand why he would ask me to wipe his glasses if he could wipe them himself. He was just sitting beside me doing nothing except holding out his glasses to me. I did what any self-respecting American woman would do, and asked, "Why? You can clean your own glasses."

In refusing an opportunity to do a kindness for him, I offended him deeply. He was insulted. We quarreled. We stopped talking and didn't talk the rest of the evening, even over dinner at his parents' house. He told his parents of my behavior, and his parents talked to both of us about understanding each other and being kind to each other. His parents were wise. We were not.

Had I understood the essence of that interaction, I might have foreseen that this marriage would not be peaceful. But life is not so obvious, nor my insight so clear; we would marry anyway.

APRIL 1984

Boston. It took a few years of back and forth, but we finally married. After the wedding we were resting in a Cambridge hotel room before the Chinese dinner banquet. One of my mother's close friends drew near me and asked, "So, how did you meet him? How did you know it would be him?" She looked at me with keen interest.

A chill ran through my body, raising goosebumps over my skin as I suddenly remembered. It was spring, in Taiwan, at a small university, five years earlier, and I was standing in the post office by the counter, next to the foreign-student mailboxes, next to a handsome broad-faced Chinese man dressed in a formal navy suit. I watched as he shuffled through envelopes to American universities, saw how the last one was addressed to my university, to the school I would return to in September. And my mind raced ahead in a second that felt like lightning: he'll go to my school, we'll fall in love and marry. I had looked for a wedding ring. None, though he looked older and was probably married and with children. I had walked away, not to remember the moment again. Until now.

I looked down at the gold wedding ring on my left hand. It had happened. I shivered.

For our first two years of marriage, I was in graduate school. Upon graduation I was offered an excellent job in New York City, so I spent the third year commuting to and from New York. I returned to Boston in 1987 to rejoin him, exhausted and worn.

I tend to think of those years as happy because, relatively speaking, in between disagreements, we were content.

At the best of times it was like this. Saturday morning, I would get up early, silently slipping out of bed, stepping as gingerly as possible to avoid the creaking of the wood down the stairs, using the downstairs bathroom to avoid waking anyone. I would wash and toast raw cashews or peanuts sprinkled with kosher salt in the oven. I would boil water for Chinese tea and to prepare dough for scallion pancakes, chop half a dozen scallions, roll out the dough, pour salt, then oil, then scallions on it, roll it up, then flatten it into a pancake for frying, then cut it into pie-shaped pieces. I would take Japanese short-grain rice and boil it in 4–6 cups of water to make rice soup, occasionally putting in small red berries or dates or raw peanuts. I would braise some tofu slices with oyster sauce on ginger slices. Fry mung bean sprouts with garlic and salt. Serve wheat gluten and pickled cucumbers, ginger and garlic.

After cleaning up breakfast, I would begin cooking beef chunks for beef noodle soup at lunch, with watercress or spinach in it. Three hours later that would be ready. For dinner I'd be back in the kitchen again to make rice with three dishes of meats and several vegetables. At the best of times we ate like this. At the best of times we ate.

At the worst of times we didn't eat. If I was exhausted from work and didn't go into the kitchen to cook. If what I cooked, spaghetti with tomato sauce or hamburgers and mashed potatoes, didn't appeal. If I miscooked or overcooked the steak or fish. If I didn't prepare a fancy meal before he left on a trip. If I didn't have rice soup and some cooling food (parsnips or bitter melon or watermelon) ready when he came back from a trip, all dehydrated and exhausted from the plane ride. If I offered sandwiches at noontime on the weekend, or worse, expected him to fend for himself—after all it was the weekend, and I thought there were more important things to do than cook three meals a day . . . wrong. If I didn't cook well or simply did not cook, it was the worst of times; not only did I not love my husband, I did not love my family, and worse, I was selfish. I was ignoring, no, willfully violating, the most fundamental tenet of the marriage: nourishing my family with food. Nothing was more important than that.

Food was the single most important aspect of family life. Food nourished us, kept us intelligent, healthy, and comfortable. If I cooked, and cooked well (tasty, fresh, well-balanced, varied), my family would be happy and well. Food, not affection, was the way of communicating love; I cook to show love, he eats it to receive it. He then works harder at work to bring home more money to care for his family and its future. At the best of times we ate.

So we did have things in common: we both loved Chinese

food. The only problem was who prepared it, how often, and how much time it took. But there were other things we liked. We liked entertaining together. We liked watching Chinese miniseries on videos we rented in Chinatown. And we especially liked talking about our friends. We talked very easily and at length about other people's romances. Both of us had mediated in several of our friends' relationships, but as far as our own, we could not discuss it at all. So when we were confidently predicting that someone else's marriage would not last for this reason or that, I was always left with an uneasy feeling that we were ignoring our own. I did not focus on what I felt, it was so clear what he felt: except for my hauling off to China and then again to New York for a year each, except for my relaxed use of money, my inconsistent preparation of food, and my very different priorities, we got along well, and we would make it.

NOVEMBER 1987

Boston. I returned from the year in New York and started a new job. In January 1988, we found a house, and I got pregnant. In October my first child was born: a son, a dragon boy. This American wife had given birth to the first son, a first son born in the year of the dragon, an auspicious start. My mother-in-law arrived in November to take care of my newborn son for six months. Her aging but still stunningly beautiful face showed a deep kindness. Barely two weeks after she arrived, my husband left for two weeks of business travel in East Asia. I was anxious. She spoke no English. But it went well, or so I thought.

We had many conversations in full Chinese, she with a slight northern Chinese accent. I learned many things about her life, her parents, her children, her faith, her beliefs. She told me of her mother's conversion to Catholicism on her deathbed, and of her own faith. I felt honored to spend this private time with her.

I was working full time, so I didn't do much shopping, just

went to work and back every day. We didn't discuss who would prepare dinner, but every evening when I returned from work, there was a delicious hot meal waiting. She found a lot of frozen turkey in the freezer and prepared a different turkey dinner each night the whole time my husband was gone. She was an incredible cook. I marveled at her variety and felt proud that we were using the turkey, which I usually would keep frozen for a year and then regretfully throw away. I felt we were living as she wanted to live, not wasting anything, being very careful about everything — from how warmly we were dressed to how we spent money and how we used leftovers.

When my husband got back, he was very distressed. I got an earful. How come I hadn't bought more meat? Were we so poor, his mother asked him, that we could not afford anything else? How come I hadn't thought more of his mother to buy better foods? What did I take her for? Why had I let her do all the cooking? It did not matter that I left the house at seven in the morning and arrived home after six each evening. I still don't think his mother complained, I think she just asked to know, but he heard it with anger.

At night I cried, feeling I had totally misread my mother-in-law's cooperation. The despair I felt was overwhelming. Night after night I silently cried myself to sleep, wishing I would not wake up in the morning.

As the days rolled forward, every night behind the closed doors of the master bedroom became the battleground for settling the score of my insensitivities. I felt a deep pain and ache in my being. How much wrong could one be blamed for, when trying so hard, and still survive sane? It was not long before I completely moved out of the master bedroom, taking my pictures and all my possessions into the extra room.

As the days continued, the frustration my husband felt at my inability to respond "appropriately" to his mother turned into rage, a rage I had never before seen in my life. It surged like a volcanic eruption, an earthquake, or a tidal wave, and felt as terrifying. I would be in shock, frozen in place, startled like a rabbit in the road facing oncoming headlights at night. His mother was calm and would try to insert some peace, but I was scared.

In public he spoke my praises: "She's traveled the world. She speaks five languages. She makes the best scallion fried pancakes. She's a great Chinese cook. Her Mandarin is excellent." At home, he was unhappy. He would read the newspaper over dinner and leave the dishes he didn't like, and ask me with a heavy frown on his brow and a deeply critical tone why I had again done something else the wrong way. More and more, he spoke of how I did things differently from the way he did and how unacceptable that was. I could not anticipate what he wanted, so even when I was trying as hard as I could to please him, I would be startled at his discontent and disappointment. More times than not, I had no strength to try hard at anything.

I had taken the serious risk of suggesting that perhaps his mother should return to Taiwan because our arrangement was so volatile, but that was a great offense. My mother-in-law did finally return home after eight months, exhausted. However, for us, the misunderstandings were so bitter that the relationship would never recover. I had suggested that we get counseling, but that too was turned down completely. I had tried countless times, in all different ways and contexts to talk it out and reach some common ground, but I learned that talk was a cultural thing. I found myself wishing my life were over, not wanting to face anyone or anything, just wanting to sleep. Coming home from work, after dinner, just sliding behind my bedroom door, lying down, and drowning out all feeling. I didn't feel I could leave; I had married for life. The days slipped into years.

JANUARY 1993

Chinese New Year. We were rushing around the house readying for a party with a U.S.-educated Chinese lawyer, his wife, and friends.

"You're not going to wear that?" he said, with the deep furrowed brow that had rarely unfurrowed in years.

"So what do you want me to wear?" I asked in frustration. This was an old battle, one I could never win because I never thought the way he did.

"Put on the red sweater and the navy pants. Don't wear sneakers."

"But you're wearing sneakers?"

"It's different for men."

"Did you get something to take to them?" I reminded him.

"Damn it. I forgot. Why don't you go down and get a pot of tulips or something to give them?"

"No, every time I do that, you don't like what I get. You go."

"Look, just do it, I don't have time. I've got to find the contract to show him."

I left the house, frustrated and defeated already. Down the small hill and past the reservoir to the family-owned farm stand I drove. Inside the plastic-roofed flower stand, I wandered back and forth, past the tulips, the hyacinths, the cacti, the primroses, the petunias, hanging spider plants, large leafy pots. Back and forth.

The tulips were beautiful and red, but they would die shortly and would need to be thrown out. The hyacinth had a very strong scent that would fill the apartment they lived in, and not everyone liked that scent. It, too, would die shortly and be thrown away. The cacti were ugly and had spines over them, not implying a friendly spirit. The primroses should really be planted outside and wouldn't last long. The spider plants were too ordinary; Chinese New Year merited a flower. Then there were the petunias. They didn't need a lot of sun and the apartment was dark. The pots were small; the window sills in this apartment were small. I could get three; three represented plenty for the Chinese. The flowers kept blooming and could live for a long time. I considered this decision for twenty minutes, precious minutes because we were running late, until at last

I convinced myself that the three small flowering petunias were the choice offering for our hosts. I drove home.

"Show me what you bought," he said.

"Here." I held up three small pots of petunias, blooming prettily in red, pink, and rose.

His brow furled deeply. "Why didn't you get tulips like I asked you?"

"You didn't say to get tulips, you said 'tulips or something.'"

"Why did you get three small pots? You should have gotten one big pot. No one gives three small pots. Why can't you just do what normal people do? I can't believe it."

I shut off the sound of his voice and his presence. I filled myself with white noise and no feeling. In silence we drove to the party with our son.

That night I stayed in the living room with the kids and started coloring with some colored markers. I began one of my long slow pictures, the ones that use the technique of multicolored strokes to create an impression. It was the ocean, a vast uncrossable ocean, with a sun rising far off on the horizon and land to one side. I drew this scene every time I stopped to draw. It was my theme, my vision, my mantra.

My son came over as the ocean was almost complete. "Here Mom, let me draw a bridge for you." He picked up the marker and drew a bridge over the ocean.

My skin rose with a chill. A bridge, a way to get from one side to another. My son had drawn me a bridge.

As we drove home, I was expecting to be scolded for not participating in conversation, for withdrawing to the living room while the others heatedly discussed the latest developments in China, job opportunities in the United States, and the experience of being expatriates. But apparently his evening was so rewarding, it didn't matter that I had cut out, and I had really cut out in more ways than he could have known. My son had drawn me a bridge to get across this vast uncrossable ocean I always drew. There was going to be a way to get to the other shore.

FEBRUARY 1993

I had been in and out of therapy for four years, thanks to the kind encouragement of a nurse at work who heard the despair in my black humor and advised me to seek help. Sitting in the therapist's office before Valentine's Day, I finally admitted that I lived in a constant state of anxiety. I connected my feeling of fear of my husband with my fear of my father when I was growing up as a child. As I said it, I felt a tremendous weight fall from my shoulders: I had no strength left to stay in the marriage. My body had given me the answer I could not get to with my head or my heart; the marriage was over. It was as simple as that.

In the next few weeks I tested this answer. I felt I was standing before a court of justice, facing a trinity of judges: my Christian values, my Chinese values, and my child's right to a home with a mother and a father under the same roof. I thought we were being true to these three values by staying married no matter how unhappy we were. But there was a deeper principle at work that I had missed all these years: marriage is sacred because of the love it bears; when it loses the grace to foster this love, it has already lost its sacredness and in substance has already ended. So I was not ending the marriage by the act of moving out or by taking the legal step of getting divorced. In fact, I felt it was not I who ended the marriage; it had ended years before when we became unable to live peacefully and lovingly together. My son's right was not to the physical condition of having two parents under a single roof, but much more importantly, to the loving, peaceful, and stable home that that implied. I knew what I had to do. I was ready to tell my husband.

He returned from business travel in March. When the time was right, I respectfully told him that the marriage was over and that I was going to file for divorce. I told him that there was absolutely nothing he could do and that I wanted to end things peacefully. He did not argue. Every few weeks he would ask whether I was still serious. I was resolute.

In June, I gave the escrow to the lawyer to proceed and began preparing the house for sale. In August, I filed for divorce and moved out with my son. In November, the house sold and I served papers. In March 1994, I resigned my job, and we went before the judge. In April, my father came up to drive me back to Washington, D.C., where my son and I would live with my mother. In June, our ten-year marriage was legally over. I had reached the other shore.

I came home to my parents' home, to the furniture, rugs, and objects I grew up with, to the food I knew as a child and the warm optimistic voice of my mother. But I am not the same girl my mother raised.

Now I speak Mandarin when I want to say something personal. I want to cook meals for those I care about; the more I care, the more dishes I imagine cooking. I tell grown men to add a sweater or jacket. I believe in the Chinese understanding of hot foods and cold foods, and matching the kind of food with the kind of stress or weakness you feel. I believe that colds come through becoming cold, despite what Western scientists prove in their tests. I cover my son's belly and lower back, knowing that's where the vulnerability to sickness comes. I make sure his head is not directly in the air currents from the window or the fan, for that will make him sick.

I will ask you whether you've eaten when you come to my home and will give you a drink even if you say you don't want one. I may exclaim in Chinese expressions and lament that you don't speak Mandarin to be able to share the pleasure of it with me. (Why should you know Spanish or French but not Mandarin?) I feel deeply that gentle humanness I felt most keenly in China. I feel it is now in me; it is in my bones, this Chinese flavor, this Chinese spirit, in my marrow.

I studied Chinese to learn what this ancient people knew, and it was very deep and very profound. But it was also very disturbing. Chinese women, like women in every culture I have known, are supposed to live for others, renouncing themselves, something I could not be happy with. How often I had remembered his words, the ones that gave me no excuse to keep him out of my life: "But, I, too, am human." These words embodied the rights to tenderness, affection, and respect: the right to be treated with dignity. How often had I said them quietly to myself, wanting to believe them. It took me years to finally hear these words deeply enough to know I had to end the marriage. I, too, was human. I had reached my limit.

WINTER 1994

We were together fourteen years in all, across continents, cultures, years. Now, all ended, but then again not. We have a son we cherish and a separation agreement we crafted together, the way we first became friends, working together over a keyboard. Even though there are enormous cultural and, most importantly, personal differences between us, we both have become better parents through the divorce because we are focused on our son's well-being. While I am relieved to be out of this intercultural marriage, I learned more from crossing cultures than I could ever have imagined.

SWAYING

Susan Tiberghien

LEARNING HOW

hen I waved goodbye, my parents said, "Don't fall in love with a Frenchman!" I laughed and said, "Of course not."

I arrived in the fall, fresh out of college, with years of French behind me, only to discover that I couldn't pronounce the name of the place where I was going. Grenoble. Or rather I couldn't pronounce it the French way. When I'd try to tell people where I was going — at le Havre where the boat docked or at Paris where I stopped en route — they would look at me and say, "*Pardon?*" They made it sound like another place. I said Grenoble, they said *pardon.*

They didn't know what I was talking about, and I didn't know what they were talking about. I kept hoping it would be a matter of weeks and I would become fluent, but it was more a matter of months. Day after day, I'd smile and listen and smile again, and every day I'd understand a few more words, and then another few.

Grenoble in the 1950s was a handsome city in the heart of the French Alps. Wrought-iron balconies decorated the facades of the gray stone buildings, and the dark red roofs slanted toward the sky. Wide boulevards crossed the city, each one ending in a snow-topped mountain. The university buildings were in La Vieille Ville close to the winding river.

I went to the registration office and learned that there were no student dormitories for girls. I was on my own, with a city map and a list of private rooms for rent. Diligently, I started with those close to the university. First I'd ask to see the room. Then I'd ask to see the bath. The landlady would shake her head, no bathroom, only a sink in a corner and a water closet in the hall. I was beginning to lose hope when finally one rather lofty lady acquiesced and showed me a grand white bathtub with lion paws. I didn't think to ask whether there was also hot water. I settled into a bare room and after bracing myself through a couple of cold baths, I inquired after hot water.

My landlady told me that there were public baths — with hot water — on the other side of the city. So once a week, with my cake of soap and my bath towel, I'd take the trolley and stand in line, waiting for my tubful of steaming hot water. Sometimes I'd fill it twice.

In the dead of winter, the water froze in the apartment pipes. We had no running water whatsoever, and, still worse, we had no heat. My landlady took to wearing her fur coat and fur hat, but I didn't have any furs. I wrapped myself up in woolen blankets and woolen socks, scarves and mittens, and tried to study. Finally, I stayed in my room only to sleep, all dressed up and wearing my boots.

I was supposed to be studying contemporary French literature. I registered at the *Faculté des Lettres* and chose courses related to the twentieth century. But I was unable to understand more than one sentence at a time, so I dropped my morning lectures to go to French classes and in the afternoon returned to the *Faculté*. This time I chose courses on the basis of which professors spoke the slowest. It didn't matter what the subject was, just how it was spoken. It was only when I found myself taking notes in French that I realized something had happened. My mind had switched to French.

However, that was only half of becoming fluent. I was understanding but I was not being understood. I could see people wince when I mispronounced a word. After much practice, I had learned the French *r*. I could almost say "Gre-noble" and gargle the *r* out correctly. But the professor said it was my nasal consonantal diphthongs that were wrong, insisting that only when I could correctly pronounce *un bon vin blanc*, would I be truly fluent. I repeated the sounds, *un, on, in, an*, until finally I was able to ask for a good white wine and be understood each time.

Next came the ski lessons. Everyone skied at Grenoble, and each Saturday the university ski club organized lessons on the mountains close by. The instructors asked me whether I had ever skied before. I nodded my head, and they put me on the cable car right up to the top of Chamrousse, where the Olympic giant slalom run was held the following year. No one asked me where I had skied or how often I had skied. They wouldn't have understood me anyway. It had been on a snow-covered golf course when I was ten years old.

So up I went to the top of the mountain. When we began putting on our skis, I couldn't figure out where to put my feet or how to work the clamps. The instructor thought I was joking. Then we started down the mountain, about ten of us, one behind the other. It was snowing and our instructor kept yelling back, *aval*, and then, *amont*. One means to turn on the upper ski, the other means to turn on the lower ski. It was snowing so hard that it didn't matter, I couldn't see the difference. At the bottom, the instructor counted to make certain we were all there.

The next week, when I went back in sunny weather and saw the slope I had skied down the week before, I tried to say there had been a mistake. I said I was only a beginner. Wasn't there another slope, lower down? But it was too late, I was already in the cable car on my way back up.

I took my meals at a student hall where the dining room was on the second floor, which for the French is the first floor. Instead of lining up downstairs, everyone would just plough their way into the wide stone staircase. At first I couldn't believe it. I thought I'd be able to help them understand how much simpler it would be to wait their turn in line. But this was out of the question, anything resembling a line was simply not French.

This particular line in wintertime, with snow and ice on our boots, was treacherous. More than once, several of us would slide backwards, only to be pushed forwards by those behind us, as if we were changing gears. No one ever really fell. In fact it became sort of fun. We would sway back and forth together.

Inside the dining room, I always sat at the same table and listened to the same group of students. They'd discuss everything with the same passion, be it skiing or Marx, noodles or Mendelssohn. There were two girls in the group and five boys. The girls mostly listened, although they had no evident problem with their diphthongs. The boys never listened; they talked all at once. Some were Catholic, others were Communist, some were both, others were neither. There was a war going on in Algeria. Some were for the French staying in, others were for the French getting out. The same evening some of them would be picketing a talk on *Algérie française*, the others would be inside listening. Afterwards we'd all go out together.

There was little pairing off and dating. When I explained how in the States a boy and girl first dated, then went steady, then got pinned, and then engaged, they wouldn't believe me. They shook their heads and said it sounded like standing in line. So wherever we went, we'd pile onto the scooters, the eight of us, the girls with their arms around whoever was in front of them.

In the evening, we'd go for coffee at La Place Grenette in the heart of La Vieille Ville. We'd order eight *café filtrés*. On top of each cup would sit a little metal filter, with very black, freshly ground coffee at the bottom and hot water on top. We would wait for the water to seep through, sometimes trying to hurry it along, most of the times forgetting it. The coffee was lukewarm at its best. We'd stay late into the night. The boys would order cognac. The girls would dip sugar cubes into their glasses, calling each cube a *canard* or a duck.

In May, over a long weekend, one of the boys in our group organized a student trip to Venice. He asked me to go along just for the company. But when I overslept the morning we were to leave, he had the bus come right underneath my window and told the chauffeur to honk the horn. The others waited patiently while I gathered my things, hurried out the door and down the dark staircase. From then on Pierre kept me up front with him so I wouldn't get lost.

On our way back we stopped to spend a day at Bellagio, a little village jutting out into the middle of Lago di Como. A few of us took a boat across the blue-green lake to the Villa Carlotta, where the azalea gardens were riotous with color and perfume.

We walked along the narrow shaded paths. Somehow in the middle of all the flowers, Pierre and I found ourselves alone. The bushes, each branch laden with blossoms, were taller than we. They opened their arms, then closed them behind us. The flowers — red, pink, fuchsia — glowed in the sunlight. Their sweet fragrance made me lightheaded.

And unexpectedly I fell in love with a Frenchman. I stopped worrying about my nasal consonantal diphthongs, they started to come naturally. And when I went back to the States in the summer, I no longer wanted to stand in line. I wanted to sway.

PRACTICING

We have an old chalet in the Alps, or rather, my French parents-in-law have an old chalet in the Alps, and they are happy to have their children and grandchildren use it. For several years my husband and I, with our six children and our dog, would leave our home in Geneva to spend the weekend in the mountains. It seemed something very French to go to the chalet in the mountains, especially in the wintertime when there was lots of snow.

Come Friday evening, I'd have the car ready and packed, so we could leave the city as soon as Pierre arrived from the office. "There's less traffic after 7:00 P.M.," he'd tell us, looking for an excuse for his long working hours. "The ride's much easier and more enjoyable."

We had the largest station wagon we could find, a Peugeot *familiale, grand format*. When we went to the mountains, I'd take the youngest child up front with me. The three older children sat on the middle seat, and the two in between sat all the way back. At first we tried to shift the children around, wanting to be fair and democratic — a little bit American — about our family habits. Then we decided it was essential to have a few strict habits, or perhaps rules, and we assigned seats according to age. "Everyone will get his chance," their father said.

The two younger ones weren't so sure, but then they had Junon, our collie, with them on the back seat. She was a rather big dog — a queen goddess, as she was named — for a crowded station wagon, but she was a good traveler. She knew that otherwise she'd be left home alone.

Each child took along his gym bag, a sturdy cloth bag that school children in Geneva used during the week for gym clothes, and which we used during the weekends for toothbrushes and pajamas. There were also six sleeping bags and a pair of sheets for Pierre and me. There were blankets at the chalet. Every weekend I'd offer to take more sheets for anyone who wanted to make his own bed, but the children still opted for sleeping bags.

Then there was the carton of food. "It's much easier to arrive with everything ready," Pierre always said. And of course, it was no trouble to prepare and pack and watch the children while he was tidying up his desk at the office. I'd try to make it all fun.

After all, it was the thing to do, go to the mountains for the weekend. The food went behind the last seat of the car because the skis went on the top, all sixteen of them, with the boots at everyone's feet, except at the driver's. I took his boots, along with my boots and youngest child's boots, at my feet.

We sang songs as we drove along. An hour's ride tended to become long and tedious when there were eight of us in the car and when we seemed to be less disciplined than Pierre remembered in his family. So I led the songs, sometimes in English, sometimes in French, and tried to keep everyone happy while Pierre drove. We'd sing "My Bonny Lies over the Ocean," and we would sway from one side of the car to the other, careful not to hit the driver.

As we got closer to the chalet, we would start singing louder and louder, giddy and excited. Even the father would finally join in. "*Savez-vous planter des choux?*" We made up the verses. "*Savez-vous faire la fondue?*" That was for Saturday night, cheese fondue, every Saturday night during the entire winter. It was the father's specialty. The children and I would grate the cheese and cut the bread. Pierre would stand by the stove and stir the wine.

When we arrived, we'd rush out of the car and run around the chalet and roll in the snow with Junon. If there was fresh snow, we'd have either to shovel out the driveway in the dark or carry everything from the road across the yard to the chalet, including the sixteen skis and the sixteen boots and so forth.

While the father and three older kids figured this out, I'd go inside with the three younger ones. Sleeping bags and sturdy gym bags went upstairs on each bed. The carton of food went in the kitchen, the boots in the cellar, and a fire in the fireplace. The house was always freezing when we arrived on Friday evening and would warm up nicely just when we left on Sunday. So we'd jump up and down, hop and skip, and the youngest children would stand as close to the fire as they dared without getting burned. They were like pieces of toast in an old-fashioned toaster needing to be turned every so often. I'd put water on to boil for pasta and warm my hands over the pot. I would have made the tomato sauce back at the house and brought it along in the carton of foodstuffs, along with the package of noodles.

The chalet was old and little mountain mice had been coming inside each winter for years. So while the pasta was cooking and the tomato sauce was simmering, I'd start to clean up after the mice. There must have been a village of them in the cellar. My mother-in-law set traps, but I never could bring myself to do it. Maybe it was because we had pet hamsters, brown and white and furry, back home, in cages of course, but still. So I'd get the broom and dustpan and then forget about them until the next week.

When the older children came in, they would set the table, using as few plates and as little silver as possible. They didn't want to spend the evening washing dishes, especially washing dishes with cold water. The hot water never got up to the faucets until Sunday, like the heat in the radiators. Instead they wanted to play outside in the dark *La Bête Noire*, the Black Beast, our favorite family game.

Even in the coldest and the darkest of nights we would play. That only made the game more fun. After supper, we would choose straws to see who would be *la bête noire*—who would hide first and be the black beast, while the rest of us tracked him down. Whoever drew the shortest straw would dress in a dark coat, with a dark woolen hat and woolen mittens, and then go outside to hide somewhere in the yard—behind the bushes, under the pine branches, alongside the back wall, on top of the woodpile. Junon would run along to keep him company.

The rest of us would count to a hundred and then pile on our coats, mittens, hats, and scarves. We'd turn out all the lights in the chalet so that the yard was inky black and so that even if we squinted real hard we wouldn't be able to see. When we were certain that *la bête noire* was well hidden, we'd follow one another outside and down the steps to the yard, holding on in order not to stumble in the dark.

We'd stomp and shout all around and make all the noises we hadn't made during the week. We'd also stomp and shout all around because we were just a little bit afraid to be outside in the dark, shooting for the black beast. But we'd never admit it, not even to ourselves.

As soon as one of us found him, very quietly, without letting anyone else notice it, we'd slip in alongside him, hiding ourselves as best we could. Sometimes Junon's tail gave us away. We'd try to hold it still. We'd try not to say "chut!" not to sneeze or giggle or make any noise. We'd clamp our woolen mittens real tight over our mouths, and we'd wait and watch as the others continued to hunt all around.

"Where are you?" they'd shout. "*La bête noire*, where are you?" We'd not make a sound, not a little peep. "Woof!" they'd shout, trying to get Junon to give us away. Soon only five or four would be left stomping and shouting around the yard. Then still another one would find us and squeeze in. "Woof," the others would try again, and we'd hold our breaths.

There would be three left, then two. This would become frightening, and we'd never let just one child stomp around for long. It was too scary to be all alone in the black, black night.

And still we'd wait.

It seemed it was always the father who was the last one out, who stomped around the yard, ranting and raging, alone. Then, of common accord, the rest of us, snug together in our hiding place, would change the rules of the game.

The father became *la bête noire*, and when he'd get close to us, and still closer, and then still closer, we'd jump out from behind the bushes, all seven of us, screaming and shouting, "*la bête noire!*"

Over the years, I forgot what were the right rules for the game. Who was the beast? The one who hid first all alone or the one who was the last to find us? I only know that each of those Friday evenings when we'd pack ourselves into the car for another winter weekend in the family chalet, I'd sharpen my claws and wait my turn with *la bête noire*.

REMEMBERING

I grew up with the stars and the moon. There were green shutters on our house, but they were only for decoration, like bright ribbons. I slept with my window wide open, watching the stars and waiting for the moon. In the early morning, I'd listen to the songbirds in the maple trees close by.

Pierre grew up with closed shutters. He slept in a pitch black room. The maid closed the shutters tight each evening and opened them each morning. That was when she would air the room, sticking the bedding out the window and bringing it in again at noon.

When we were first married, we didn't pay much attention to the windows and shutters. We were living in the States, close to my parents' home in New York, on the second floor of a large yellow clapboard house that had no shutters, no green ribbons. Pierre was studying and I was teaching. Our days and nights were full, and we gave no thought to the missing shutters.

Then we moved to France, into his family's house. There were no longer any maids, and his parents had transformed the servants' quarters on the top floor into an apartment for their oldest son and his American bride. The windows had heavy wooden shutters. Pierre showed me how they worked. He said it would be his job to close them each evening and open them each morning.

Sleeping in complete darkness was something new. I missed the sky and the cool air. I'd wake up in the early morning and sneak to the window trying to open it just a little and let in some light and air, but the little slits on each shutter were slanted at such a degree that nothing got through. I decided to be patient. We weren't going to be living in his parents' house forever. In the meantime, I'd open wide the windows during the day and sleep with fewer covers during the night.

Our own first house in France was in a little village in Provence. We lived on the ground floor, and there were only two windows, each with simple shutters that even I could close and open. I learned that all France closed its shutters, not just my husband and his family. At night no lights could be seen in the entire village. Everything looked deserted. Windows were blackened and I learned to blacken ours.

I never tried putting the bedding out the window. I had brought American linens with me across the ocean, sheets that were lightweight and easy to wash. They were half the size and weight of the sheets Pierre had grown up with — embroidered damask, extra long to wrap around the fat bolster pillows. When we went to bed, he would try to keep them tightly tucked in place. But beds tended to be very narrow in France, and when I'd loosen the sheets on my side of the bed, they'd slide completely to the ground on his side.

Fortunately, his first job took us to Belgium, a more neutral country for a French and American couple. We rented a second-floor apartment in a row house, with wide windows in the front and back, and gray metal shutters that rolled up into gray metal boxes at the top of each window. There were handles to make them function, hanging on long arms along the side of each window. The handles had to be grasped firmly and shaken into place, otherwise the arms remained limp in the middle.

We were living on a large avenue in downtown Brussels. There were lights at nighttime and the houses no longer looked empty. But our bedroom was in the front of the house, above the din of the street and traffic, so I didn't yet suggest that he change his childhood habits. But I did start letting in a little fresh air once he was asleep. I'd slip out of our bed and grope for the long-armed handle, trying to shake it noiselessly into place and then to rotate it, raising the shutters — there were three of them — just a crack. I'd fall asleep instantly from all the hassle.

Next we moved to Italy, a country still more neutral for us, with another language. There were again shutters, *i scuri* in Italian, instead of *les volets* in French. They too rolled into boxes, but with easy cords to make them work. And there was a half-way position, with the bottom half of the shutter slanting outward. The Italians left the shutters in this position all summer long during the day to keep out the hot sunlight.

We celebrated our sixth wedding anniversary and decided to try keeping the shutters in the half-way position during the night. We were living in a large white apartment house high on a hillside, far from any city and from any main road. I once again felt fresh air on my face and listened to the birds in the early morning. And there was something new, the perfume of flowers. Our Italian neighbor grew roses, fragrant pink roses on bushes as tall as little trees. All night long their fragrance filled our room.

When Pierre's work moved us to Switzerland, I thought our nights with open shutters had been successful and would continue. But our first apartment was near the Geneva airport, with planes flying in and out all night long. Back we went to closing the shutters, as tight as possible.

We also went back to our one-arm bandits, the same limp arms hanging to the right of each shutter. I still had trouble making them work. When our oldest children started manipulating them, and then when all six children could flip them into place within seconds, I realized there must be something in my genetic makeup that prevented me from coping with shutters, be they French, Belgian, Italian, or Swiss.

After a few years, we moved to a house on a quiet street, a house full of windows and full of shutters — old-fashioned wooden shutters, ones that latched shut. The house was in the middle of a large yard, with hedges all around. Every night I'd open the windows and shutters an inch wider, slowly accustoming my unsuspecting husband to sleeping with a little light and a little fresh air.

And to my surprise, and still more to his surprise when he learned my secret, Pierre continued to fall asleep just as easily and as soundly. I reveled in the cool semidarkness, feeling free and unfettered. Sometimes I'd quietly get out of bed and walk around the house, all alone, enjoying the obscurity and the freshness of the night.

Then it happened. I awakened one night to a full moon poised in the middle of our bedroom window. I remembered back to my childhood bedroom in New York, when I used to look out my window at the stars and the moon. I woke up Pierre. From our bed, we gazed at the round ivory moon, its light illuminating our room, our covers, our arms.

And now, every night, we sleep with the shutters and windows wide open. Once again I watch the stars. I wait for the moon, and when it comes, big and ripe and milky, I wake up Pierre and we watch it together.

NOTES ON CONTRIBUTORS

CATHERINE CASALE graduated with a B.A. in history from Tufts University and left the United States to work in Japan. She worked in publishing for several years in Japan and England before earning an M.A. in Southeast Asian area studies with a focus on economic history from the University of London's School of Oriental and African Studies. Her essay is excerpted from a book in progress. She recently moved with her family to New York from Japan.

JUDITH ORTIZ COFER was born in Hormigueros, Puerto Rico, and immigrated to the United States in 1956. She has published several books of poetry, among them *Terms of Survival* (Arte Público, 1987); a collection of essays, *Silent Dancing* (Arte Público, 1990); and a novel, *The Line of the Sun* (University of Georgia Press, 1989). Her most recent book, *The Latin Deli* (University of Georgia Press, 1995), is a collection of stories, essays, and poetry.

NORA EGAN is a Massachusetts-born writer who grew up overseas in many different countries on the Mediterranean. Her essays have appeared in the *Global Nomad Quarterly* and *Notes from a Traveling Childhood* (a Foreign Service Youth Foundation book). She lives with her son in Maryland.

FAITH EIDSE was born and raised among the Chokwe-Lunda people in Kamalaya, Zaire, and among the Mennonite settlers of Manitoba, Canada. She obtained a B.A. in English from Eastern Mennonite College in 1979 and worked as a newspaper reporter and editor in Canada and the United States. She obtained an M.A. in creative writing at Florida State University in 1995 and has been published in various magazines, newspapers, and literary journals, including the *International Quarterly*. She lives with her husband, Philip Kuhns, and sons, Anthony and Stefan, in Tallahassee, Florida.

JESSIE CARROLL GREARSON earned an M.F.A. from the University of Iowa Writers' Workshop and an M.A.W. from the University of Iowa Expository Writing Program. Her poetry, essays, and reviews have appeared in such publications as the *Christian Science Monitor, Iowa Review,* and

Yankee Magazine. She works at the John Marshall Law School in Chicago, where she helps law students learn to write more clearly. She is currently working on a book of nonfiction about living in an intercultural family. She lives with her husband, Viren Sapat, and her daughter, Emma, in Evanston, Illinois.

MARY HANFORD was born in Washington, D.C., and grew up in Europe and the American Southwest. She is an English professor at Monmouth College in Illinois and has an interest in African studies. She taught in Cameroon for two years and in 1995 directed a program at the University of Zimbabwe. Her poetry and short stories have appeared in the United States, Africa, and India. Her book, *Holding to the Light*, was published in 1991.

LE LY HAYSLIP is the author of two books, *When Heaven and Earth Changed Places* and *Child of War, Woman of Peace*, which together were made into a film by Oliver Stone. She founded East Meets West, a non-profit relief and world peace organization. She lives with her three sons in southern California; her son James Hayslip helped her write her memoirs, from which the essay in this collection is drawn.

FERN KUPFER is an associate professor of English at Iowa State University in Ames, Iowa, where she teaches and directs the creative writing program. She is the author of three novels; a nonfiction book, *Before and After Zachariah*; and many articles, short stories, and essays. Her most recent book, *Love Lies* (Simon and Schuster, 1994), is a mystery novel. She lives with her husband, fiction writer Joseph Geha, and a blended family of daughters.

ELIZABETH MARTINEZ was born in the north of England and brought up in Surrey. After completing a B.A. in combined studies (English, theology, and social sciences), she worked in libraries and publishing. In 1989 she moved to Switzerland to join her Argentinean husband, and there she began working as a secretary at the United Nations. She now lives in France with her husband, a classical musician, and their son.

CHRISTI MERRILL is a Ph.D. candidate in the Department of Comparative Literature at the University of Iowa. She is also a freelance writer and a translator; most recently, she contributed translations to *Survival: An Experience and an Experiment in Translating Modern Hindi Poetry* (New Delhi: Sahitya Akademi, 1994). She spent the 1994–95 academic year on a fellowship studying in India.

LITA PAGE is a freelance writer now based in the Southwest. She has lived in Asia, Europe, and South America.

RUTH PRAWER-JHABVALA has written many novels, including *Heat and Dust*, which won the Booker Prize for 1983. She is known for her work with the award-winning Merchant-Ivory team of filmmakers; her screenplay for *A Room with a View* won an Academy Award. She lives in New York City and in Delhi.

JOANN HANSEN RASCH teaches, writes in her journal, and occasionally publishes stories and essays in magazines and anthologies. She is now finishing her Cambridge Diploma for Teaching English as a Foreign Language and living in Lutry by Lake Geneva.

LAUREN B. SMITH earned her M.F.A. and Ph.D. from the University of Iowa. She teaches multicultural and writing classes at Eastern Illinois University. She commutes between her home in Champaign-Urbana and Whitewater, Wisconsin, where her partner, Hassimi Traore, teaches chemistry. She is currently working on *Acts of Love*, a book about feminist theory.

SUSAN TIBERGHIEN, wife-mother-grandmother, is a freelance writer living in Geneva where she edits a literary review. Her stories and essays are published in periodicals and anthologies in Europe and the United States. Author of *Looking for Gold* (Daimon Press Zurich, 1995), she is working on her own collections of intercultural stories.